UNSPOKEN

Toxic masculinity and how I faced the man within the man

HarperInspire, an imprint of
HarperCollins Christian Publishing
1 London Bridge Street
London SE1 9GF

www.harpercollins.co.uk
www.harperinspire.co.uk

First published by HarperCollins 2021.
Copyright © Guvna B (Isaac Borquaye)

Guvna B (Isaac Borquaye) asserts his moral right,
to be identified as the author of this work.

A catalogue record for this book is available from the British Library

ISBN: 9780310112020 (TPB)

ISBN: 9780310112471 (ebook)

ISBN: 9780310113584 (Audio)

Typeset by e-Digital Design

Printed and bound in the UK by CPI Group (UK) Ltd, Croydon CR0 4YY

MIX

Paper from responsible sources

FSC   FSC™ C007454

FSC™ is a non-profit international organisation established to promote the responsible
management of the world's forests. Products carrying the FSC label are independently certified
to assure consumers that they come from forests that are managed to meet the social, economic
and ecological needs of present and future generations, and other controlled sources.

This book is produced from independently certified
FSC paper to ensure responsible forest management.
For more information visit: www.harpercollins.co.uk/green

UNSPOKEN

Toxic masculinity and how I faced the man within the man

GUVNA B

INSP:RE

To my dad, Charles, and my son, Ezra.
With each generation, there is as much
to learn as there is to teach.
Love you both. x

CONTENTS

INTRODUCTION

Toxic Masculinity: *A cultural concept of manliness that glorifies stoicism, strength, virility, and dominance, and that is socially maladaptive or harmful to mental health.* (Dictionary.com)

In 2017 my world turned upside down when my dad died suddenly and unexpectedly. One moment he was on the L-shaped sofa watching *Match of the Day*, full of smiles, and the next day, gone, vanished from my world. I was twenty-seven years old and had never taken a moment to consider my life without my dad by my side. His death plunged me into the depths of despair, where I lost all sense of who I was. I felt lost and alone, and lacked the necessary tools for coping with a bewildering sense of grief.

All my life I have struggled to communicate, but with the death of my dad, my inability to impart how I was feeling had a massive impact on my mental wellbeing.

As a black man of Ghanaian origin raised on a London council estate, many of my influences conditioned me to believe that boys don't cry, that men are tough, that we can handle ourselves through thick and thin, and that we are immune to every emotion. The disadvantages we faced left no room for emotions to delay our progress. I was also unable to share how I felt as I was scared of being judged, of being seen as weak, and vulnerable, and out of control.

It was my struggle to communicate in everyday conversation that initially led me to songwriting and I am eternally grateful for having had the opportunity to turn both this need and passion into a living. Known professionally as 'Guvna B', I am a rapper, the recipient of two MOBO awards and three Urban Music Awards. My music has amassed over twenty million streams. At the time of writing, my latest album, *Everywhere + Nowhere*, is the highest selling 'clean' rap album of 2020, and I have over 100,000 followers across social media. Even though writing music is my 'exhale', the release of all the pent-up thoughts in my head, I've always felt that the influence I've gained through music can be used for even greater things. I have always sought to offer positivity through my lyrics, to break down the stereotype of rap music as centring only on drugs, sex, and violence, and to share hope and inspiration.

It was only after my dad died, however, that I learnt how to truly express my pain and to face the man I was within.

I had to. My survival depended on it.

What I was not expecting was the overwhelming response I received for my honesty, at opening up and revealing my defencelessness. The messages I received were full of heartfelt thanks, largely from young men, for 'telling it like it is', for showing them that it is okay to bare their souls, that vulnerability, fear, and anxiety are human traits that affect us all, regardless of our gender.

My dad's death marked a turning point in my life. By removing the blinkers from my world and the world around me, I was granted a new sense of purpose – the purpose of helping those around me to cut through the conditioning that comes as part and parcel of being male, and to help young men obtain the courage to open up and expose the fragility lying just beneath the surface.

I am not an expert on mental health, or grief, or youth violence. I don't have any formal qualifications to write about these subjects, but what I do have is several years' worth of word-of-mouth and hands-on experience, in addition to caring deeply about these topics. This book is aimed at all young people, but as a black man, I know about the trials and tribulations that black men face in trying to carve a path in an already overcrowded white person's world, and I write from a black man's perspective. I ask questions relevant to young black men, start the necessary conversations that concern black men, and listen to what young black men have to say.

As a man of faith, I have always felt the need to help other people: I see it as my God-given purpose to do good in this world. Although my music is my passion, I place great value on the work I do mentoring young people. I joined the Eastside Young Leaders Academy and mentored secondary school kids when studying for my degree, and I have continued mentoring ever since. Through my charity, Allo Mate, I provide opportunities for aspiring young musicians to launch their careers in the music industry; I am deeply involved in my work as an ambassador with the overseas development charity, Tearfund; I present a podcast called *The Loss Tapes*, on grief and its impact on mental health; have given motivational speeches at venues such as Wembley Arena and the O2; and work as a broadcaster and documentary presenter for the likes of the BBC, on matters relating to music and young people. This book is an extension of the many conversations I have outside and alongside my music career.

Knowing that I can make a difference in young people's lives is my inspiration for writing *Unspoken*. I see this book as an older brother – an older brother cares; an older brother protects; an older brother is relatable; and an older brother is further along the path. The older brother knows that there is likely going to be a moment in your life when you come face to face with who you really are. I had that moment and it took me a long time to set myself straight. I don't want you to have the same experience. I'm not even fully straight yet – I'm kind of like a bendy ruler.

In this book, I dig deep to discover the man within; and I learn that only by being honest, and attuned to my emotional self, have I got a chance of cutting my teeth in this world – a world where survival does not rest on being the toughest, but on knowing who you are and having the confidence and the courage to show it.

1. FIRST-GENERATION BRIT

I was born Isaac Charles Bortey Borquaye on a council estate in East London. My parents moved from Ghana to England in their early twenties with hopes of starting afresh and creating something meaningful for themselves and their children. Hard work was in their DNA and every fibre of their being was dedicated to building something substantial and sustainable.

I'm a first-generation Brit and so were many other kids in the area. It was such a diverse place to live. We had working-class English people who had lived on the estate for generations, as well as Ghanaians, Nigerians, Algerians, Jamaicans, Dominicans, Portuguese, Polish and so many more, whose parents had moved to call this place 'home'.

'Immigration' is often a divisive word, but on an estate like mine, it united people, gave them common ground to stand on and build from. There were many conversations that showed we were all different, but in a lot of ways, all the same.

At the time, I thought my mental and emotional states when growing up were excellent, but the person I am today agonizes for the teenage Isaac. The truth of the matter is, I was emotionally debilitated, with melancholy filling up my days all too often. Pinning that down to one reason is tough, but first-generation Brits from a working-class background know that growing up in a deprived area comes with many problems, which don't always present themselves as negative.

As I attempt to peel back the layers, the way I have come to understand my emotional immaturity is the fact that, when I was growing up, there wasn't time to express emotions. My parents were on a mission to further the legacy of our family. They had given up familiarity, the home they knew, being close to their family, being comfortable with the ordinary and everything else, for this opportunity. There wasn't any way that emotion was getting in the way of that. Their hunger for greatness was infectious and something they passed onto my younger brother and me.

When I put myself in their shoes, I get it. They were in a fight for survival. At one point we lived in a single room with little money for basic household needs. They didn't have time to sit down on a regular basis and discuss in a healthy way how they felt about the situation. They were too busy trying to make the rent that month.

I had an abundance of aspiration in my household, but a lack of it on the estate from my peers. We lived from day to day. We didn't really wake up and think, *I have a purpose and I'm going to work towards that today*. I guess most of us never saw past the estate. It's weird when I think about it because *The Fresh Prince of Bel-Air* was one of my favourite shows. Every day, at 5 p.m., I'd come home from school and it would be on the television. I'd see Uncle Phil and Auntie Vivian's big mansion and all the resources they had for their family, but not once did I think that was something I could attain. Not once did I think America was even somewhere I could go. We rarely saw past the estate, but then again it's hard to visualize something you haven't personally experienced. One of the only youth clubs in the area got shut down so we'd just hang around on the streets or on the communal green, and then we'd go home and see our parents struggling to make ends meet.

We started to think that this was all life had to offer and didn't share our feelings often with those close to us because things weren't likely to get better so what's the point?

Another layer was toxic masculinity, which was rife. I remember having a fight when I was about twelve years old with a guy who was a couple of years older than me, over a silly PlayStation game, and a heated argument got out of hand. I was punched in the face and it hurt obviously, and pain plus extreme anger can result in tears. I remember the guy asking, 'Why are you crying?' I'm guessing because it hurt?

The message that something like that sent out was that even if you're in pain and, even if you felt like it, you didn't dare cry because *we don't do that around here*. This became problematic when friends from the estate lost their lives to youth violence and we didn't grieve properly, because we didn't do emotion. We suppressed the sadness, the hurt, the loss; and life, seemingly, went on.

We're all conditioned in some way, shape, or form and that's something to bear in mind. We're conditioned to behave in a certain way or accept certain circumstances. It's the reason me and my friends viewed success as being the local kingpin of the drug trade rather than the guy we saw suited and booted walking to the train station at 8 a.m. to start his job at JP Morgan. The kingpin wore Nike Air Max 90s. The three-piece suit and Oxford shoes of Mr JP Morgan cost more than the Nike trainers, but we didn't care – success looked like Air Max 90s to us.

Why was that?

Conditioning.

If you were to ask me how I'd describe myself, it would be laid-back, logical, and a man of faith. I definitely get the laid-back nature from my dad. He had a spot on the L-shaped sofa we have in the front room. Whenever I walked into the house, I could bet my last pound he'd be chilling in that spot watching Formula 1 or an African soap of some sort. In earlier years he'd have the Teletext screen on and just read that. How weird! I'm probably showing my age, but you can Google-image 'Teletext' if you're not familiar with it. Anyway, the point I'm trying to make is he was very, very chilled; cool as a cucumber in Antarctica. I don't remember ever seeing him act erratically or show his anger externally. Living life that way seemed to bring him peace and that kind of tranquillity is something I aspired to. I remember making a vow to myself to hold things lightly and not allow myself to get worked up, so that I could maintain my peace like my dad seemed to do so well. I figured that I couldn't always control what people did to me, but I could control how I responded to it.

The need to constantly improve on myself is my logical nature. My life is busy and I only have limited brain capacity, so if I want to keep my sanity, I have to compartmentalize. This way, I ensure I only worry about what I need to worry about when it becomes a worry. I am often accused of being so logical that I come across as emotionally distant and unable to empathize with the people closest to me. People say, 'You need to let off steam, Isaac', but in truth, it's my logical nature and ability to see the big picture that keep me on track.

I am often asked how I can be logical at the same time as carrying a strong faith: 'Surely the two are incompatible?'

The way I see it is that my faith requires no analysis. It's not something I choose to opt in or out of. It's a part of me, as dear to me as my heart and lungs. I get that it is not logical to believe, but where God is concerned, there isn't always a time or place for logic. My faith is my lifeblood and my belief non-negotiable.

My parents are Ghanaian, and Christians too, so that usually means we children go to church as soon as we depart the womb, whether we like it or not.

Though I was heavily persuaded to go, I became mature enough over the years to develop my own thoughts and ideas on what I believed. I doubted the Church on various occasions, but for some reason I never doubted God. It wasn't a theological epiphany or spiritual awakening that made me feel this way, just a feeling I always had. I'd look at withering leaves or the detail on both of my palms and think to myself, *I think someone created this. I think there's a mastermind behind the undeniable beauty of the things my eyes witness.* Ultimately that led me to a journey I'm still on and even though having faith doesn't exclude me from the issues that may turn up at my door, it provides comfort knowing that I don't feel like I'm alone. I walk confidently in that and it became a big part of my identity. So much so, that I actually felt the need to live up to the chilled and faithful persona I thought I had been blessed with. This meant that in confrontations or difficult conversations, I would back down even if it didn't feel natural and even if I wanted to fight my corner. The person I wanted to be was more important than the person I was.

I remember when my faith became part of my identity many of my friends started behaving differently around me. At first, they thought maybe it was a phase that I would come out of at the other end. When this didn't happen, I noticed that they adopted more of a positive attitude, stopped using bad language, and took me more seriously. I had one friend who was notoriously badly behaved, always getting into trouble. No one knew why he conducted himself like he did as he never let anyone in. One day, he took me aside and began opening up like I was his confidant. When I realized what was going on, it was a bit of a lightbulb moment as I saw that my faith could be a force for good. People appreciated my world-view and found it comfortable being vulnerable around me. It also placed me under quite a lot of pressure to live up to my identity: to carry myself in the correct way, be well mannered, trustworthy, and stand up for what I believed in.

I told you before that people know me professionally as Guvna B. You might be wondering where the name comes from. It comes from school where me and my friends used to give each other military titles as tag names. I was 'Guvna', then there was 'Lieutenant', and 'General'. We were an army of friends. Truth is, I never would have called myself Guvna as my working title if I had known I was going to be a successful musician, but it just kind of stuck from school. And the 'B' is for Borquaye, my Ghanaian surname. As for my two middle names: Charles was my father's first name; and Bortey is a Ghanaian name and means 'first-born'.

So yeah, that's me. Professionally, I'm Guvna B – rapper, writer, broadcaster, and mentor; but at home, I'm Isaac – husband, father, son, and brother. My identity is forever evolving, but my heart is firmly established with my family and with God.

2. MY DAD

My parents brought me up to be different which, for the duration of my childhood, I struggled with, as fitting in was all that mattered to me. I wasn't allowed to do any of the social activities my friends got up to like sleepovers, parties, or staying out past sundown. I had to be home safe, where my mum and dad could see me. Now, I get why they treated me like this – they wanted the best for me. They didn't uproot themselves halfway across the world just to see me and my brother fall into bad ways and be stranded by the wayside. They had dreams for us … ambition. They were intent on us fulfilling our potential and that meant staying on the right side of the tracks and, more crucially, staying alive.

I was born in Barking Hospital in June 1989, and the first fourteen years of my life were spent living in a council flat on the Bridgeland Road Estate in Custom House – second floor, Red Block. The flat overlooked the Custom House DLR station, along with a small playground, and row after row of identically shaped council blocks, distinguished only by colour. My friends inhabited Green Block next door and Yellow Block opposite, and this relatively cocooned neighbourhood formed my early life.

In my house it was my mum who ruled the roost. She was the one who was there to make sure my brother, Joel, and me got up, did our chores, and came home on time. She was the one with the plan. That doesn't mean my dad didn't share the vision for our futures; it was just that my mum made it happen. When my mum set her mind on something, she went for it. My dad, brother, and me all accepted that this was how it was and none of us rocked the boat.

I remember one time when my brother and me were watching TV and Mum called up from wherever she was – out shopping most probably, at the old shopping centre in Stratford, as those were the days before flashy Westfield moved in.

'I'm back in three hours, Isaac. I want you to tidy the kitchen and Joel needs to take the meat out of the freezer so that it can be defrosted by dinner.'

'No problem, Mum,' I said.

As soon as the phone call was over Joel and me were instantly transported back to TV Land. The next time I looked at the time, over two hours had passed and my mum was due back in twenty minutes. My brother and me moved like the wind. Joel grabbed the meat and I tidied that kitchen top to bottom. When my mum walked into the house minutes later, she prodded the still rock-hard meat and fumed at us for not instantly heeding her words, so we were grounded for a week.

That was my mum. As I told you, she was Queen Bee.

It was most probably because she was such a doer that my dad was happy to sit back and take whatever came his way. His motto should have been, 'Anything for an easy life.' Don't get me wrong: he was laid back not lazy. Every day at 5.30 a.m. he would be up, brushing his teeth to go off to work. I used to wake up too as the bathroom had paper-thin walls and was right next door to my bedroom. I remember I used to lie in bed and wait for the small gag that always accompanied the brushing of his tongue.

Happy days!

My dad came from Kokomlemle, a district in the Ghanaian capital, Accra, and spoke the dialect Ga, which is the ethnic tongue of the city. My mum came from Darkuman, twenty minutes west (if there's no Ghanaian traffic), and spoke Fante. Both of these languages were spoken at home, along with English, and now that I have a child of my own, who I can share my roots with, I am grateful that they passed these dialects on.

As the eldest of three children, I suppose my dad was expected to be the adventurous one. He wanted a different path and to make a life for himself elsewhere. He came over to London on his own, but when he was settled, he sent for my mum to join him.

After my dad died, I went to Accra with a group of close friends to celebrate my thirtieth birthday. I had been a few times before, but never with any attempt to see the city through the eyes of my dad. I suppose you could call it a 'journey of exploration', on which I tried to get a sense of who my dad had been. I admit, I didn't know much about him when he was alive, as it had never crossed my mind to ask. I had only ever seen my dad as *my* dad, not as an individual in his own right. It didn't help that he never spoke about himself. Correction: he never spoke at all much, beyond one-word answers.

During my trip, I learnt that growing up, my dad had been streetwise and assured; never one to draw attention to himself; understated but coolly confident. I liked hearing these things about my dad because it confirmed how I thought about him too.

Turning up for the first time in London, I expect he lost some of his assuredness, as it must have been a massive culture shock. I wonder if he felt like an impostor, like he shouldn't be here, and didn't fit in. That would go some way towards explaining his passive nature – don't ruffle feathers, keep the peace, and don't give anyone any reason to tell you to go back to your own country. Live and let live and, most importantly, laugh. Or maybe those features were just what made my dad who he was: easy going and happy-go-lucky.

My parents' first job in London was to work as cooks at Harrods. To their families back home, hearing the word 'Harrods', it must have sounded like they'd hit the big time. In reality, it was a tough job made up of long hours and little pay. Food and cooking formed a massive part of my childhood, always chicken and jollof rice, or plantain and beans, so it's funny when I think of my parents preparing traditional British munch like roast beef and Yorkshire pudding. That said, my dad often used to cook us a top-notch full English breakfast.

That fact my parents were the strictest parents of all the kids around made my life difficult. Their hard-and-fast rules and unbending discipline created a mass of internal tension that I just had to bear because the other option – disobeying them – was a far more terrifying prospect. If I did something wrong my mum shouted at me and threatened me with whatever object was nearest to her. She loved me deeply but that was her default. She always acted on impulse, whereas my dad was measured, but drove his point home. The funny thing is, I don't actually think my dad was that strict but went along with it for the sake of my mum, as sometimes I'd say to him, 'Why do I have to, Dad?'

And he'd kiss his teeth and reply, 'Because.'

Trying to argue a point with my parents was a waste of time because what they said went, even if it lacked any kind of logic. That's child-rearing Ghanaian style: children are expected to respect their elders, no ifs or buts, and in the confines of my home I was 100 per cent Ghanaian. My dad used to say, 'Outside the front door, that's London. Step inside and you're in Ghana.'

At school was where I let out all my frustrations. School was my release, the place where I could kick back, argue, swear; best of all, break the rules. Being brought up differently from my friends meant I had to work extra hard at fitting in. I didn't want anybody knowing I was different. Where I lived, being different made me a target. I craved my schoolmates' respect, which is why I took it upon myself to be the class clown. This was my only option for being seen. Though I loved sport, there were kids way sportier than me and although I could be tough, I had my limits. As for matching the Cool Crowd on a material level ... forget it. That was why I was always messing about and getting into trouble. But I wasn't scared of my teachers: nothing they said could touch me. All of my fear was reserved for my parents.

Reading this, you're most probably thinking, *Wow, those parents!* Don't worry. My parents loved me. Growing up, I never wanted for anything. We had very little, but they never put across any sense of a hard life. Food was abundant and their love overflowed. But it was *tough* love. I always used to joke that the only time my dad ever spoke to me was either to say, 'Isaac, you need to *be* somebody', or to tell me off.

His telling-off normally revolved around my schoolwork, whereas my mum stuck to telling me off for not doing my chores. Yeah, I was a lazy child and my mum didn't like having to tell me more than once.

It was because my parents expected so much from me and my brother that at home I sometimes felt like I was at risk of drowning beneath the weight of their expectation. It was hard to dissociate myself from machine or robot: I felt like a barcode indistinguishable from any other barcode, existing only to serve a function. Don't get me wrong, I wanted to succeed. Who wouldn't? But my parents were pushing me down a path that felt miles off the track I wanted to go down, which was, at the end of the day, the same track as all my friends.

We never did traditional mealtimes at home, where we sat around a table and made conversation, which on the one hand, I deeply regret – I will get to why later – but on the other hand, I am very grateful, because my parents would never have let up. For as long as the meal lasted, they would have been on at me to *work hard*, to *get the best grades*, to *be the best*.

In my parents' view, education was everything, and in those rare moments when education snuck out for a breather, in ploughed the traditional job: 'You gotta make something of yourself, Isaac'. *Making something* meant becoming a lawyer, a doctor, an engineer … jobs that were equated with success. My parents were terrified that I would waste the opportunity they had created for me.

Luckily, I had no intention of doing this, not only because I didn't dare upset my parents, but also because deep down I was aware of the enormous sacrifice they had made on my behalf, and I never wanted to let them down.

The strange thing was that while they were intent on pushing the headline advice – 'Get good grades, Isaac. Be the best!' – my mum and dad never went deep on the finer details, like *how* to get the grades and *how* to be the best. Their mentality boiled down to 'Do as I say, not as I do'.

My dad was educated, but I wasn't a fan of his teaching style. Offering patient, coherent guidance was neither of my parents' strong points. Let's say my dad was trying to teach me 2 + 2.

'What's 2 + 2, Isaac?'

If I didn't know the answer, he wouldn't break the sum down and explain it, he would just shout louder:

'WHAT'S 2 + 2?'

I still don't know, Dad.

Away from my studies (or lack of), my dad and I always got on, because we understood each other. Although he cared deeply for the wellbeing of his family, making ends meet, and his legacy, he also cared deeply for *Match of the Day*, and so did I. Some of my happiest times with my dad were watching the football. When I was young, I supported Manchester United, but when Joe, one of my best friends, started playing for West Ham, I shifted allegiance and became a Hammer. My dad was an Arsenal fan at first, but moved to Chelsea when Roman Abramovich took over. I told him he couldn't do this, but he didn't care. Brazen behaviour!

My dad was a man's man – most Ghanaian men are. It is a typical feature of our African heritage and he expected my brother and me to follow suit. One of the most stifling aspects of being *manly* was being told I was not allowed to cry. Ever.

Men don't cry.

Fact.

I was smacked as a child by way of punishment and the worst thing was that, if I ever cried, my mum or dad would smack me a bit harder. They wanted me to be strong and crying was not a sign of strength. I never felt threatened and I understood it as tough love, but still, it was debilitating for me because sometimes I wanted to cry, I *needed* to cry. But instead, I learnt to suppress it, told myself it was wrong, and fought against it. All my childhood, I believed that crying was wrong, which came to have a perilous impact on my future mental health.

Though there are deep-rooted issues from my childhood that I've had to grapple with for most of my life, when I think back, the majority of my memories are happy ones. My mum is the most loving and caring person I've ever met. There may have been better ways in which she could have done things, but she was someone who wore her emotions on her sleeve. You could feel that when she was happy and you could feel that when she was angry. I'm sure that's why my dad was such a peacemaker. He must have learnt early on in their marriage that letting any anger roll off him and never forcing his own opinions would be the best way to go. After a hard day's work, kicking back and relaxing was his sole aim, and he knew that it was easier for him to control *his own* emotions than to attempt to control my mum's.

Unfortunately, this came across to my mum as if my dad didn't care, which served to ramp up her discontent even more. At the time, I remember feeling relieved that my dad opted for calm, but now I think about it, he could have done more to help her manage her emotions.

Woah! Hit the brakes right there! *He could have done more to help her manage her emotions*? Rewind that last line. That's *me* speaking after two years of counselling. The fact that ways of managing emotions even existed would not have crossed my dad's mind; even if they'd flickered into his imagination, he would never have considered them. As I told you, my dad was a man's man and men's men never delved into their psyche for answers. He might delve into God's psyche as he could relate to the power of the spirit, but that was about the extent of his delving. As far as my dad was concerned, my mum got emotional, he stayed calm, and there was nothing deep or complex about it.

In reality, the reason for my mum's emotional state was because she suffered from anxiety. She still does and, understandably, it's been hard to manage since my dad passed away. She used to worry all the time that me or my brother would come to some harm. If she asked us to be back home at 6 p.m. but we were ten minutes late, she would worry that we'd been stabbed or something untoward had happened. This anxiety would sometimes manifest as anger. It was because of her anxiety that she used to pick me up from the train station even though it was only a few minutes away.

I found that the only way I could keep a handle on my mum's anxiety – and maintain my own sanity – was to tell her little white lies to calm her spirit. I know that my dad did the same. His role as husband was largely to reassure.

'Nothing to worry about, Vivian.'

Where my mum was a handwringer, my dad was unflustered; where she was loud, he was quiet; and where she was impassioned, he was reserved.

I took after my dad. We both shared the same number of emotions – zero. At least, that was how home life and society had conditioned us to be. That's why I still look back on those three words I said in the last hours of my dad's life with amazement and gratitude – 'I love you' – and, more importantly, why I hang onto the fact that he repeated those same three words to me.

My mum used to tell me she loved me most days of my life, so, guess what? I knew it. My dad, though ... well, I've given you a hint of how much my dad used to speak, and let me tell you, three words in a row for him was verbal diarrhoea.

I remember one time I went with my dad and my best friend, Nick, and his dad to the Royal Albert Hall to see George Benson in concert. This was a few years ago, and I had known Nick since sixth form, so my dad and Nick's dad also knew each other pretty well. Throughout the course of the evening, my dad said a total of about ten words – ten! – and even that might be pushing it. He had a great time, I know that because he smiled and laughed, like he always smiled and laughed, and he loved George Benson, but literally no words came out of his mouth.

For the majority of his working life my dad worked as a warehouse manager for French Connection. All of his ambition, hopes, and dreams rested on my brother and me. He needed us to do well, as we were living proof of his having made the right decisions and chosen the correct path. Many of my friends didn't have dads in their lives and suffered the consequences that accompany abandonment: lack of a solid male role model and discipline. I am very grateful to my dad for always being there, but I don't think he ever grasped how debilitating his rules and outlook were on my ability to fit in. The truth is, he never had time to contemplate. Fitting in didn't matter to my parents. In fact, in order for their hopes and dreams to come true, they relied on us *not* fitting in, as fitting in meant potentially going down bad paths and not making a success of our lives.

Children never really value their parents, not until they have children of their own and come to understand how hard it is to be a parent or, in my case, until one of their parents dies and they become aware of the enormous hole in their lives.

Something my dad always did for me, without fail, was to drive me places. As I grew older and my career took off, he drove me to all my gigs and when I was touring, it was my dad who drove me to and from the airport before I could afford airport parking! I really miss sitting next to my dad in the car. We never said much:

'How was your tour?'

'Fine.'

That was pretty much it, but we sat in comfortable silence. Beside my dad, I always felt secure. I knew that he had my back. Sometimes we'd laugh. Laughing was the glue that held us together – laughing and football. Like me, my dad loved jokes, but he was rarely the joker. While I attempted to be the class clown when I was young, as I got older I had to accept the fact that I was never the funny one in my crowd. Other people were always quicker off the mark than me. I could be funny, but my jokes normally came to me several hours late. They were funny jokes as well – or at least they would have been two hours earlier. My dad was just content being a listener. With his self-assuredness, he didn't need to be the popular, funny guy.

Anyway, the reason I am telling you this is because, thanks to my mum's anxiety, my dad's silence, my suppression of crying, severe impostor syndrome (inherited from my dad maybe, but more likely, based on my own insecurity – I'll get to that) – and my inability to fit in, I grew up completely lacking the tools necessary to communicate my feelings. My mum used to practise soul-searching: 'Are you okay, Isaac? What's wrong?' But I knew that as much as she cared for me, it was simply to calm her own nerves. If I was fine, she could relax; and I was always fine, remember.

Growing up, I never saw my insecurity as linked to any of the above. It was only later on, when my survival depended on my ability to tap into my emotions, that I realized how stunted I was in this department. Until faced with adversity,

I never knew that vocabulary existed for logging into one's mental state. Also, I have to admit that, back then, I was never one to look at the big picture. I lived in the moment; saw only what lay in front of me when it took centre stage. My life revolved around what Isaac wanted there and then, and 366 days out of 365, that was trainers.

Yeah, I wasn't a deep kid. I wanted those black Air Max 97s more than I wanted breath in my lungs. Okay, that's maybe a slight exaggeration, but I was so desperate to buy them that, with the £2.50 lunch money my dad gave me each day, I bought sweets to sell to my schoolmates. I used to believe that if I owned a pair of £120 trainers, my life would be complete – forever.

Guess what? I never got those Air Max's. My mum wasn't interested in my consumer needs, so I settled for a fake pair from Wembley Market: thirty quid they cost me and they looked almost identical to the real deal, so I could have pulled it off, but I couldn't lie to myself and so, in my head, they never counted.

I did eventually get myself a real pair, but not until I was a grown man and they came back into fashion again. I didn't even really like them any more. I bought them simply because I could and they reminded me of my progress. What hadn't been attainable before now was.

Did it feel good?

A little, but by then, the novelty had worn off a bit – a bit like the soles on the fake pair from Wembley two weeks after I'd bought them.

Truth be told, I had wasted a lot of my childhood wanting the unobtainable, when the unobtainable was really not worth wanting in the first place. I tried advising my young cousin not to get caught up in the whole consumer culture, as it would only make him feel hard done by, but he just looked at me as if to say, 'You don't get it'.

So, I let it go. He had to figure it out for himself. Like we all did.

This wasn't the only time my mum took note of my need to fit in. When I was younger, I was desperate for a Sega Mega Drive. My mum bought me a Sega Saturn instead as she found a good deal, but she tried to fool me into thinking it was the Mega Drive. I'd seen the box though, so I knew exactly what it was. It was painful at the time, but now I appreciate that she tried.

During my childhood, owning stuff and being liked by the popular crowd was all that mattered to me, which is sad really, as I never got to own anything I craved, and I was never part of the popular crowd. I was always out on a limb, circling on the outside, waiting ... hoping that someone would spot me and allow me my moment to shine.

The laid-back me stems partially from those years of hiding the eagerness I felt inside. It became my trademark, which I was prepared to adopt mainly because every other personality trait – confidence, being funny or alpha – had been taken by more confident, funny alpha boys. Being laid-back is not a trait that I admire about myself, which is strange, because I admired it in my dad. It seemed to suit him because he came across as being so comfortable in his skin. For me though, it felt like I'd pulled the short straw and been lumbered with the donkey.

My default states of mind were passivity and rage. There was nothing in the middle. Rage rarely reared its head as it took a lot for me to get to that state, but when it did, mainly as a result of not being able to express my feelings, I used to lose control. I remember when I was fifteen years old, there was a party that I really wanted to go to, but my parents wouldn't let me. To their faces, I accepted their decision, but when I got into my bedroom, I was so angry that I kicked a hole in my bedroom door. My parents were completely surprised at what I had done, as I had given them no indication of how strongly I felt. The same happened once at school, when I began kicking desks and throwing chairs. Whenever I succumbed to my rage, people were shocked as it appeared so out of character.

'See? This is why you need to go to church,' my mum would say. Oh and we did. We'd all put on our Sunday best and head along to Calvary Charismatic Baptist Church in Canning Town. African people like to present their best selves to God and to one another. I was always told dressing up on Sunday was a mark of respect to God, but I am quite certain he doesn't mind what people wear.

Much like all my childhood learning, church was just something you had to do.

'Why?'

'Because.'

No reason was ever given and so I just went along with it. The music touched my soul; the routine was an essential part of my week. I met up with a lot of my friends and I knew God loved me, but I was still to be convinced by the whole idea of religion. Why go to church to feel close to God? It didn't make sense. And my parents never offered any enlightenment, because it was just what we did.

For the majority of my childhood, I went to church because I had no other choice. When I was in my teens and my parents eased the pressure, I thought, *I'm not going to do this any more if I don't understand what it's all about.* And so, I did my own reflecting and in time, built my own personal relationship with God. From that point on, I went to church not just *because*, but because I wanted to.

As I told you before, we never sat down together around the table at my house for mealtimes. For a start, we didn't own a dining table because we were in a pretty small flat. I never even realized eating around a table, as a family, at a certain time, was something a lot of people did, because my mealtimes were different. The way I grew up, there was always food cooking on the hob. Whenever we were hungry, we would go over to the pot and help ourselves. I ate most of my meals in the company of Trouble TV or Nickelodeon. In fact, the only time my family ever came together at home as a unit was at Christmas or when my mum had one of her *epiphanies*. When this happened, she and my dad would join Joel and me in the front room. They would force us to unglue our eyes from the television and request that we bow our heads and pray. Prayer sessions tended to end with my parents breaking into a badly sung song, generally a Ghanaian hymn, causing Joel and me to raise an eyebrow at one another from beneath our bowed heads.

Ghanaian Hymn

Mi jie Oyi, Nunts, mi jie Oyi
(I praise You, Lord, I praise You)
Moko b ni tam Bo
(There is no one like You)
Y nileeŋ, y sum, y fo, k hewal
(In Wisdom, in love, in beauty and strength)
Nunts, moko b ni tam Bo
(Lord, there is no one like You)
Mik mitsui baa kanfo Bo
(With my heart I will praise You)
Mik migbee baa jie Oyi
(With my voice I will praise Thee)

Mik mijwmo k lala
  (With my mind and song)
Baa jie Oyi daa k daa
  (I will worship You every day)
Hallelujah
Moko b ni tam Bo
  (There is no one like You)

That was family time – Borquaye style.

When Emma (now my wife) and I started going out, I realized her family did things very differently. On accepting the invitation to go to her house for dinner, I had no idea of what it entailed. It was a lot more daunting than performing to thousands of people, I must admit.

So, sitting around the dining table, there was Emma, her parents, and me. What you've got to bear in mind here is that I hate talking about myself. I know this might come as a shock, especially as this book centres around me and my life, but physically opening my mouth and speaking words about me does not come naturally. But this is what 'eating together' is all about, isn't it? Sitting around a dining table you talk about your day, share your views, listen to each other, define your role within the family, and master the art of conversation.

What was clear to me after that evening meal at Emma's house was that, in my family, we never really talked and, as a consequence, we never shared. And as a result, I never mastered the correct art of conversation.

I now know that if I had grown up making conversation around a dining table, I would be 100 per cent better at opening up and talking about who I am, and that would have made a major difference to my life.

3. INFLUENCE

I told you already that growing up, I felt like I didn't count, as if my life was meaningless because meaning centred only on fitting in, and that was never something I achieved. In my young form, it looked to me as if everyone had a characteristic or skill that guaranteed them an identity – everyone who mattered at least. But I had nothing.

I was caught between a home life where the word 'failure' was not an option, where I was comprised neither of flesh nor blood but of parental aspiration, and wider society, where I was just an anonymous East London estate kid lacking purpose and doomed to fail.

My school was St Luke's Primary School in Canning Town. Here, away from the savvy law of the street and the more stifling law of my parents, I adopted the role of 'class clown' as a cry for help, a call-out to be understood. The only problem with being class clown is that I made a bad impression on the teachers and was earmarked as a troublemaker. I don't know what trajectory I might have gone down in my school life, but I doubt it would have been positive if, aged seven, I had not experienced the first of two life-changing moments.

My head teacher, Ms Aanonson, called me aside one day

after I had been messing about in class. I was expecting to get the standard rebuke, 'You need to behave, Isaac,' to which I would have hung my head sulkily and nodded, before nonchalantly walking away and ignoring every single one of her words.

But I got something else instead.

'I don't see why someone as good at English as you feels the need to cause trouble in class,' she said.

'Good at English?' These words hit me like a bullet. I was stunned. Too stunned to process them.

'What do you mean, miss?'

'What I mean, Isaac, is that you have a real gift for storytelling. Do you enjoy writing?'

'I–' The truth is, I'd never thought about it.

Writing was something I did at school because I *had* to, not for pleasure because I *wanted* to.

'I'm giving you permission, in your next writing project, to write whatever you want, and I know you will do it well,' she said.

I grew three foot in the course of that conversation. It was as if I had just been handed a one-way ticket to the stars. I don't think I walked home from school that day. I floated. And it took just two words to get me there: 'good' and 'gifted'. Ms Aanonson changed my life. She had detected part of the identity that I had been scrambling around trying to locate.

From that point on, as 'Isaac gifted-writer Borquaye', I thrived in my English class and grew to love writing. I wouldn't yet say that I had found a way of expressing my true self, but it put me in touch with the rhythm of words. I used to walk tall in my lessons, with my head held high, and I never ended up in Ms Aanonson's office again ... okay, maybe once or twice more.

For the first fourteen years of my life, I lived on the second floor of Red Block in Custom House. Many of our neighbours were related to my parents either by blood or background, and so I had a lot of friends who I classed as *family*. We used to play outside together, knocking on one another's front doors to see who was available to come out. The majority of the kids were also friends from church and youth club, two very big parts of my life. As I grew older, the majority of my social life revolved around youth club. Every Friday evening, along with around twenty other kids from the estate, I used to travel to the youth club base in Plaistow on the 241 bus and play football and music, and hang out. It was my lifeline for staying on the right track. I would meet up again with the same people I went to youth club with at church on Sunday morning, so they constituted a massive part of my life.

For my first six years, I was an only child. I never felt like an only child in those early years because our house was always full of relatives, friends, and cousins. Ghanaians are very sociable by nature. Home life revolves around food and music. It would be considered the height of rudeness to have someone turn up at your house and not offer them a meal.

Loud music played night and day, which is why 'home' to me is associated with music. The Afrobeats of Ghanaian highlife music are embedded in my DNA. There are so many tunes I hear played nowadays that send me straight back to Bridgeland Road. Most of the time, it would be Ghanaian highlife, by artists such as Daddy Lumba, which was the music played at the hall parties of my youth. Or we'd have Motown: Tina Turner, Whitney Houston, Luther Vandross, Kool and the Gang; or Kirk Franklin (see picture 1), Ron Kenoly, or Mary Mary singing gospel tracks. The television would often be on at the same time, even when no one was watching it, battling for attention, although the music always won out.

> Chuffed. I get to open up for one of my musical heroes tonight. Definitely a birthday to remember. I'm on stage just before Kirk Franklin at the Copperbox Arena in Stratford tonight. Come down!
> (Instagram, 13 June 2015)

My parents treated *me* differently from my contemporaries, and *they* also behaved differently from their contemporaries, as they didn't just dream about what life might be and talk about it, they made it happen. At least my mum did. My dad's nature was never to sweat the big stuff. In fact, I'm pretty certain that he would have remained living quite contentedly in our council flat his whole life if it hadn't been for my mum's stubborn determination.

With the Government's Right to Buy scheme, my parents saved up to buy our flat from the council. This put them on the housing ladder, which was my mum's primary goal and a marked assurance of their success.

Although I was brought up living under the illusion that money was plentiful, the reality was that, at times, it was tight. Sometimes my parents went without in order for me and my brother to eat, but this was never something we were aware of. For instance, for the first decade of my life, I was pretty unaware that life existed in the form of detached houses and leafy gardens. I only became aware of 'how other people lived' when my parents decided not to send me to St Bonaventure's, the local secondary school, where all my schoolmates were going – and where I wanted to go – but instead, sent me to St Edward's School, a seventy-minute bus ride away from Custom House, in Romford, Essex.

This decision was made based on my mum's anxiety that if I went to the local school, I would come to some kind of harm, which would all too certainly lead to an early end.

The fact my parents would think of removing me from everything I comfortably knew to place me in a leafy, middle-class suburb sums up their unfaltering conviction that I was going to make something of my life, and that it was their role to ensure I had all I needed to make it happen.

What they most probably chose not to dwell on too much, was that a big part of the danger did not exist in the school grounds but right outside their front window on the estate. It was there, aged eleven, that I was first shown a gun. I remember weighing it in the palm of my hand and thinking, *How did I get here? Keeping this gun in my hand a while longer means going down one path, whereas handing it back and walking away means going down another.* It didn't take me long to decide my path as, thanks to the strength my parents had instilled in me, I had the confidence to know that the gun-toting trail would never be the one for me. Besides, the thought of my mum discovering the weapon in my bedroom drawer was a worse punishment than any kind of damage it could do. I'm pleased I was faced with the choice though, as it provided me with the opportunity to decide.

St Edward's School, Romford, was my first insight into the world outside of my East London hood and opened my eyes up to a whole other way of thinking. The most striking difference was that the school was roughly eighty per cent white and predominantly British. This was in complete contrast to my ethnically diverse school in Canning Town.

Growing up, I had never been aware of the colour of my skin being different. I looked like the majority of the people on my estate and in my school, church, and youth club. As

I have already mentioned, my favourite TV show was *The Fresh Prince of Bel-Air*, and I didn't look all that different from Will Smith – tall, dark, and remarkably handsome. I digress.

At secondary school, though, I was in the minority. As I had never really been exposed to racism, it took me a while to work out that the way I was treated from time to time was nothing to do with *who* I was, but a consequence of the colour of my skin. Racism isn't always someone calling you the N-word; sometimes it's covert and difficult to prove. Ex-American basketball player Kareem Abdul-Jabbar said, 'Racism ... is like dust in the air. It seems invisible – even if you're choking on it – until you let the sun in. Then you see it's everywhere.'

I might be walking down the street and someone would shout out of a moving car. My first thought would be to look around to see who they were shouting at. When I realized that it was most likely me, it would take me some time to figure out why they might be shouting, as racism never immediately came to mind. There were also occasions in school when I got a harsher punishment for performing the same *crime* as my white classmates. I remember letting it go as I thought the teacher must have made a mistake, but with the passing of time I am now aware that it was probably intentional.

I also had to contend with the matter of the gap between my two front teeth. Since growing my adult teeth, aged around seven or eight, I'd had a gap. I knew I had it, but never thought much about it, especially as none of my friends ever seemed to notice it. In Ghanaian culture, a gap between the two front teeth is a sign of great wealth to come and so, if any comments *were* made, they were generally made in a positive vein.

That all changed when I got to secondary school and

some class joker decided to start poking fun at 'the gap'. I've always liked humour in most forms and so I found it quite funny at first, but after it went on and the jokes escalated to the point where they were on the cusp of bullying, it began to wear on me. There was one time when I was on a station platform with a group of school friends waiting for a train. As the train pulled into the station and the doors opened, the announcer's voice came up over the Tannoy:

'Boarding this train, please mind the gap between the train and the platform. Mind the gap.'

For once my mind, usually slow to process, moved at the same split-second speed as my friends and I felt myself shrinking into my shoes at the same moment that the laughter exploded from their lips. They all began pointing at my teeth and shouting, 'Mind the Gap.' It was completely humiliating, but I had to laugh along to make it look like I didn't care, otherwise they would have seen it as a weak spot.

It was at times like this that my laid-back attitude came in handy, as it enabled me to come across as *unbothered* in the face of their taunts. There is nothing school kids like more than a riled victim. I would love to say that I shouldered all the jibes and just shook them off, but I didn't. I gave into the bullies and begged my mum to let me have braces. She was reluctant at first, as she could see nothing wrong. But she relented in the end, as she became aware how much my teeth were affecting me.

An orthodontist issued me with a retainer, which I wore for a bit, and it began to work its magic, but after a while, I decided to stop wearing it. Knowing how easy it was to close the gap removed the necessity to do it. Before it had felt like I had no choice, but once the choice had been granted, I decided to maintain the status quo. And I'm pleased that I did, because my gap has become a defining feature of who I am.

This track gives you a pretty good flavour of my home life:

Home (E16)

I grew up in E16
I was chilling on the block with a 99p ice cream, back
    then it was actually 99p
And then I played football on the green
Me and the boys played out all day till mumsy called
    names from the window, dinner was ready
Jollof rice
I was involved
man, you wouldn't believe
All the beef on the ends
And the goons in the Benzes
Look at them wrong and you might catch two left
    hooks in your lenses
But me?
I tried to do the right thing
Inside my yard
Man I was too busy writing bars
And man I went hard

I'm sitting in E16 with my headphones on, when my
    mum said, 'Dream
Cos I feel like you wanna waste your life and I just
    can't let that be.'
And I'm praying because somebody said that he's got
    plans for me.
Don't waste my time. Come, change my life. Oh won't
    you, please.

In 2003, when I was fourteen years old, my parents left the estate, remortgaged our flat, and bought their very first house. This was in the slightly more affluent suburb of Chadwell Heath, thirty minutes from the estate and much closer to my school. My mum wanted the house so much that the seller ended up giving her a £40,000 discount as he couldn't bear to break her heart.

Being one of the first families to get off the estate was another example of the way my parents inhabited a different mindset from a lot of their friends, as they were always looking for ways to progress. I remember the huge amount of pride I felt living in a house, which even though it only had three bedrooms, felt like a mansion to me. And what I loved best of all, it had a garden.

With the move to Chadwell Heath, it definitely felt like we were going up in the world – not all the way up, but definitely advancing. My mum went from working six days a week to five, the downside of which was that she had more time to pay attention to whether or not my brother and I had done our chores.

When we moved into the house, we bought a dishwasher and I was over the moon about this because by then, it felt like I had committed months of my childhood to washing and drying dishes by hand. I was all set for lazy days ahead when my dad announced that, despite owning a dishwasher capable of making dishes sparkle better than the work of any tea towel, nothing was going to change. For some illogical, irrational reason that I can only imagine was linked to power play, he wanted my brother and me to continue washing and drying by hand.

'Why?'

'Because.'

The hardest part of this whole waste of my life was that

for my mum and dad the dishwasher proved revolutionary. After installing it and using it themselves, they never looked back: further proof of my parents' strict adherence to the code of 'Do as I say, not as I do'.

When I was sixteen, I experienced my second life-changing moment. It is astounding how far one can propel oneself when fuelled by self-confidence. That one comment bestowed upon me by Ms Aanonson back when I was seven years old had carried me all the way through primary school, keeping me on the straight and narrow. This time, it was my youth leader who changed my life and put me on the path that would change me forever.

Like many young kids I had dreams of becoming a rapper, although I didn't ever think they would come to fruition as they were so far out of kilter with the dreams my parents had in mind for me. Also, like most of the kids I grew up with, I craved the gangster lifestyle – at least I thought I did: the car, the girls, and most of all, the money. To me, success equalled material wealth, which equated to a glamourous life, adorned with status and respect. Of course, I wanted all these attributes without having to go through any of the hard graft to get them.

In the world I grew up in, where money was tight but the need for respect relentless, 'G-checking' was commonplace. The gangster in each of us was under 24/7 surveillance. What did we own? Who did we listen to? How would we react in specific situations? Victim or victor? This is where masculine toxicity came to the fore.

I've already told you that crying was forbidden in my home. Well, on the street, it was *outlawed*.

Emotion has no place on the inner-city estate, where you are forced to grow up fast, due to the bombardment of life in its basest form. Knife crime has soared in the last few years and nowadays it makes the news frequently. But where I was brought up, it was commonplace to carry a knife and the consequences bled into every aspect of our lives. Although there were few fatalities among young people back then, violence was always there as a threat. Nowadays, it's got out of hand. Young people left behind after their friend dies on the street are too ill-equipped to process their grief, too tough to admit their true feelings, and too undervalued to talk about it. As a result, they become desensitized. The pain is locked away only to rear its head further down the line in debilitating ways.

This is the reality for thousands of young people. We live in a throwaway culture: one kid's life here today, gone tomorrow, but in the meantime, life goes on, but I can still relate to that sense of life lacking all meaning. Looking back, I realize now that this was the reason why getting noticed was essential to me. I needed then – and I still need now – to matter.

When I was twelve, my school had a talent show, which I decided to take part in and so I copied down all of the lyrics from Ms Dynamite's verse of So Solid Crew's song 'Envy' and I performed them to my whole school. (In my humble opinion, it's one of the greatest verses of all time by the way!) After the concert, everyone kept coming up and congratulating me on the lyrics, which they thought I'd written myself. I suppose that's a benefit of going to a school in the suburbs, where they're not as well versed in rap music. That said, it put me in a really hard situation.

1. Own up; or
2. Go and write some lyrics of my own.

I went for Option 2 and started some serious songwriting, although I didn't write anything as good as that Ms Dynamite verse for a while.

Envy
So Solid Crew
Ms Dynamite

When I step up on the microphone
Explosive people love to pimp
And play like they know dis
But they never seen the dynamite get ferocious
Yes to show dis watch while I blow dis
From I step up on dis MC ting here good vibes I try to bring
I try to fling
But it's time to show I'm not playing, be on the mic
   when I chat
But I know what they saying

A couple of years later, my youth leader, Hafis Raji, called me over at youth club and said he'd heard some of my music on Myspace.com.

'It's not you,' he said.

I was taken aback, as I was expecting some kind of praise. I was, after all, a *gifted* writer.

'You need to write what you know.'

This advice from someone I admired came as a surprise, as it had never crossed my mind to write from my own life experiences. All the best-selling rap lyrics centred around misogyny and swearing, money and violence. That had to be what people wanted. How was my reality of church and youth club, faith and strict parents ever going to appeal to an audience?

'Try it,' said Hafis. 'You've proved you've got talent. Now write some music that's true to who you are.'

When I hesitated, he added, 'Isaac, people are going to like what you've got to say.'

Hafis had played a big part in my decision to become a Christian in my own right; that is, not because my parents wanted me to be a Christian, but by carving out my own relationship with God. I don't remember the specific moment this commitment happened. It was a slow transition prompted by a sermon I heard in church on what being 'lukewarm' looked like. I didn't warm to *lukewarm*. It was too wishy-washy, so I forced myself to pick a side.

That was when I chose God, the start of my Christian journey, and Hafis was beside me every step of the way, which was why I trusted him.

He challenged me to write a song to perform at the youth club.

It was a massive challenge, but I was up for it, because Hafis had seen something in me and I needed that validation.

Although the writing, rhythm, and feel of the music came naturally, digging deep for truth was a whole new experience. What I realized early on is that if I was going to write rap from the heart, God was going to need to play a starring role, as God was my reality.

I never knew that rapping about faith existed. In fact, I was naive enough to think that I was the first person to attempt it. I mean, Kanye West had a huge hit with 'Jesus Walks', which I seem to have conveniently forgotten about at the time. But when I started looking around, I realized that there were a lot of rappers inspired by God. Philadelphian rapper Japhia Life, for example, put out a sick album called *Fountain of Life* ('sick', by the way, is slang for 'excellent'), and there were other similar albums: *Moment of Truth* by Da

Truth, and *Rebel* by Lecrae. All of these lit the path for me.

I eventually wrote a song called 'Looking out the Window', which took me six months, but Hafis was true to his word and provided me with the opportunity to perform it to my youth club. It was my first gig ever, and eighty people watched me. I was so nervous that when I was handed the microphone, it slipped straight through my hands and landed on the floor.

My performance could not have gone much worse than it did. Not one of those hours spent in front of the mirror at home practising my rapper hands paid off, but I can still recall the exhilaration as I left the stage.

That was the point when I realized I wanted more.

I bet you're wanting me to share the full lyrics to 'Looking out the Window', aren't you? I'm not going do that. Let's just say, they weren't my finest, but here are a few lines to give you a taste:

> I'm just looking out the window and I see the shining.
> Sometimes it's shining, but sometimes it's not.
> Still, I'm not compromising.
> I see to my left it's temptation and to the right it's the
> fight for the right thing.

A year later, aged seventeen, I released my first album, *The Narrow Road* (picture 2), written in secret in my bedroom at home, when I most probably should have been studying for my A levels. I saved up the money to record the album from the combination of my £30–a–week Education Maintenance Allowance (EMA), granted to young people from low-paid families to encourage sixth-form attendance, and from saved-up birthday and Christmas money.

The recording studio was based in Thornton Heath, a

one-hour, twenty-minute train ride from my home. I chose to go there as I wanted to work with audio recording and mix engineer Wayne Hermz, as he had recorded the album for the MOBO award-winning rap group *G-Force*, who were pioneers of positive rap music at the time.

The Narrow Road was a work of love. I wrote it because I needed to get the words out. I wasn't expecting anyone beyond my friends and youth club to listen to it, but that didn't stop me pouring hours into making it as good as I could get it, as I had this voice inside my head saying, 'If you work hard, Isaac, you can achieve good stuff.'

Some days I got to the recording studio at 10 a.m. and didn't leave until 4 a.m., getting a couple of hours' shuteye on the sofa. I think it was because he saw how hard I was prepared to work, and that I was putting every bit of money I was earning into the album, that Wayne developed a soft spot for me and offered to help by putting me in touch with artists and promoters on the music circuit.

I was really grateful for this, but still I didn't have any high-reaching expectations for the album, besides getting it recorded.

I decided to hold the gig for the launch of *The Narrow Road* at my youth club. I imagined around eighty people might show up, like before, but somehow word had got out. When I walked onto the stage, there were 800 faces there to greet me. I was blown away. I had to restrain my jaw from dropping to my knees. Something wasn't right. They couldn't have all been there to hear me rap! Was I at the wrong venue?

This was a surreal and massive moment. When I got my head around the fact that they were there for me, I thought, *Okay, if I can get through this, I can get through anything.*

When my show finished, two people came up to me from

London-based management company Black Grape Global. They had got word of a young musician playing positive rap and wanted to come and listen.

We arranged to meet up in a few days, for a chat about representation.

Just that meeting alone would have had me punching the air for days to come, but walking home from my gig that night, I had more immediate matters to deal with, primarily the £4,500 sitting in my pocket from that night's sale of CDs – £4,500! I had never seen that kind of money in my life.

All right, so, the sensible thing would have been to put that dough straight into making a video to expand the reach of my single 'Kingdom Skank', as it had been selling really well.

But guess what?

I didn't do that.

My parents had always said to me, 'Don't get involved in selling drugs.' And I never did. Instead, here I was with legitimate coinage burning a hole in my pocket and I wanted to show people that I could make an honest living.

So, I took that £4,500 and I went to Stratford Shopping Centre, and splashed out on trainers, tracksuits, and a whole load of other bits and bobs that would elevate my status directly from schoolboy to kingpin.

Two months later, unsurprisingly, the money was all gone, every last penny, but I didn't mind, as I now had the means for making it all over again, as I had signed a contract with a management company and they had big plans for me.

By taking that leap of faith, Hafis had shown me the way. If he had not challenged me to write a song true to my soul, I would most likely still be writing inauthentic gangster rap and wondering why no one was interested in my music.

Having people believe in me changed my whole view of

myself, but because I was insecure, my impostor syndrome was through the roof. As time went on, I found myself dragged down by the belief that perhaps I shouldn't be making my music, that I had no right to be up on stage performing, that sooner or later, someone would discover that they had put their faith in the wrong person. I was waiting almost daily for the phone to ring and for someone to say, 'Sorry, Isaac, big mistake,' even after I started building a fan base.

It was funny though, because while I was feeling like the great pretender, with my fear of failure enabling me to function at only seventy per cent of my capacity, my music was gaining in popularity. Through all my years of wanting desperately to fit in and be a part of something, here I was – the square peg, away from the crowd, carving out a direction that didn't 'fit in' with the mainstream. People were responding to my positive lyrics. This was surprisingly liberating. There was no sense of expectation as no one had gone before, and no direct competition beyond the need to improve daily on myself. What's more, I was now setting a path for others to follow.

Young Isaac, the class clown, could never have imagined that.

Do you know what motivated me most back then, and still does now to a point? It was watching the audience transform from sceptical – Who *is* this Guvna B? – to grateful, joyful even, as my music triggered a chord or nurtured a need. Knowing that just by opening up my heart I could connect with so many lives was my fuel.

I have often wondered whether the reason I felt like a fraud was because nowhere on my parents' list of 'traditional jobs for a successful career' was the word 'rapper'.

In their eyes, who actually made a living out of exciting

a crowd through their music? All their working lives my parents had toiled, day in day out, to give my brother and me the best life possible. Was I letting my parents down?

If my GCSE grades were anything to go by, then the journey of disappointment was already well underway. To this day, I never have admitted to my mum that I dropped out before retaking my GCSE Maths, so if she's reading this, 'Sorry, Mum.'

My AS levels were even worse, which was hardly surprising as during my first year I was busy writing and recording, keeping it a secret from my parents, and during the second year I was promoting it. I didn't tell Mum about the £4,500 I earned, but I did tell her about my management contract.

Of course, she kept me grounded: 'That maybe the case – you can be Guvna B outside – but at home, you're Isaac and you will do your chores.'

To my parents, my music was just a successful hobby; something to do to pass the time as I prepared my life for my all-important professional job.

Somehow, despite my grades, I managed to scramble a place at the University of Hertfordshire. In my first year there, I studied Computer Science, more to appease my parents' desire for me to do something worthwhile than for any deep-rooted interest of my own. I did dismally in the end-of-year exams. So much so that it was recommended that I pick a new course, which is how I got to study Business and Journalism.

That was a great move, as I loved the idea of learning how to write for lots of different audiences, so I saw it as another string to my bow. What I learnt from the course was that writing in my own voice is where I am most comfortable. Putting lyrics down on paper is how my brain strings thoughts together. It's funny because rap was never my favourite kind of music to listen to – I much preferred UK garage, gospel, or old school – but rap just happens to be the music I am good at writing.

I remember when I was in secondary school, we were sometimes sent to the school library to pick out books for literacy studies. I could never find any books that spoke to me: none of them were anywhere near where I was at, except for Benjamin Zephaniah's rhyme books, like *Funky Chickens* and *Talking Turkeys*, along with his poetry anthologies. By writing in my own voice, I find I can communicate directly with people who might otherwise feel underrepresented in the world of writing.

Despite having a 'gift' and the capacity to connect, I didn't really believe that music was a viable career either, which is why, after leaving university – and in between writing and performing my music – I got myself a 'proper' job working for the phone company O2 as a salesman, selling phones and contracts.

I was really excited at being offered this position as, aged twenty-one, it gave me the chance to make money while working my way up a career ladder. What's more, it turned out I was good at it, as I had the gift of the gab and was skilled at building a playful, mischievous rapport with the customers.

Achieving Salesman of the Week for selling the most contracts was a huge accomplishment, as was earning the recognition and respect of my boss.

Everything at O2 changed one day, however, when an elderly lady came into the shop. That particular week, we were meant to be pushing the new iPhone to customers, but it was immediately apparent that this lady had no need for such a multilayered device. I sold her a different type of phone that better suited her needs, but when my boss found out he was fuming. When it came to the end of the week and I had not met my target, he tried humiliating me in front of all my colleagues by showing them my stats. I remember sitting there as he was belittling me, thinking, *You know what? I don't need this.*

It was like a spark suddenly ignited in my brain: *If I'm good enough to succeed at this job then, with time and effort, I'm good enough to succeed at anything.*

I didn't hesitate: I walked out of the shop there and then. It felt great. I most probably punched the air or something. As I drove away though, I was hit by panic.

How was I going to make money now?

A day or so later, I went out to my car to put a bag in the boot. Inside, scattered all over the floor of the boot, were loads of £2 coins – some of my earnings from selling my CDs at all my gigs. I looked at the coins and thought, *I really need to start treating my music business with a little respect.*

Up until that point, music had been a side thing, a passion, but never a serious job. As I gathered up the coins, I made the decision to give it a go: to put my music first and to do everything I could to turn it into a living.

It turned out to be a pretty good decision and I have never looked back.

4. GOODBYE

'He'll tell you it's nothing,' my mum said, opening the front door to me as I arrived at my childhood home in Chadwell Heath. 'But I'm worried. He's just not well.'

'I'm sure he's fine,' I said adopting the same reassuring tone I had heard my dad use countless times when my mum's anxiety levels were spiking.

'Of course, I'm fine,' came my dad's voice from the front room, where he was laid out on the black leather L-shaped sofa, legs up, TV on, dressed in his customary jeans and T-shirt.

'Dad's always fine,' I said, although I was surprised to see him looking more subdued than normal. Usually my arrival triggered a wide smile, but he seemed barely able to raise his head. I wasn't at all worried though – my dad was a strong man.

'You say he's fine, but look at his neck.' My mum pulled my dad's T-shirt aside to reveal a series of lumps. *That doesn't look right*, I thought, but I didn't voice this out loud, because I knew my mum had called me around to alleviate her fears, not add to them.

'I'm sure he's fine, Mum.' I said this because I knew it was what she needed to hear. 'You both just need to keep an eye.'

We left my dad sitting in his favourite chair and I went into the kitchen for a bite to eat, unable to resist my mum's cooking.

Life had been exceptionally busy lately, as I was putting together the finishing touches to an album I had been working on for several months.

A little while later, belly full, I left Chadwell Heath and made my way home, pretty certain that my dad was most probably just a little run down from working too hard, but more relieved that I had been able to soothe my mum of her concerns.

I thought nothing else about it until the next day, when my mum called to tell me that she was taking my dad to the hospital for them to run some tests.

'Are you really that concerned, Mum?'

'Yes, I am. He's still no better.'

My mum might have been anxious by nature, but I did trust her instincts, as it had been her decision twenty years before to call for an ambulance – against my dad's wishes – when he had experienced shortness of breath. Then, he had ended up on the operating table having an artificial valve inserted into his aorta during open-heart surgery.

So, that had been the right call.

My mum called a few hours after they left for the hospital, telling me my dad had been discharged but then readmitted after feeling faint, and so was having an emergency biopsy on the lymph nodes on his neck. Hearing this, I got into the car and drove over to the Queen Elizabeth Hospital in Romford, grateful that the medical team were taking my dad's condition seriously. But I still wasn't too worried as my dad was fit and, at fifty-eight, he was still relatively young.

What I did want to do, however, was to check that he was bearing up and, perhaps more importantly, to make sure that my mum was coping.

When I got onto the ward, my dad was there, propped up on his pillow, with a drip in his arm, eating some dinner. He looked washed-out but smiled and looked as much like my dad as he ever did.

That evening, I had a show in Bristol but was uncertain whether or not to go, as I didn't want to leave my parents. I could tell that my mum was a lot calmer now that my dad was in the safe hands of the hospital, and so heeded her words when she told me to go and that they would both be fine.

The next morning, I went back to the ward. Catching sight of my dad in his NHS gown attached to a drip in a hospital bed, I was struck for the first time by his vulnerability. In the twenty-seven years that constituted my time on earth, my dad had always been my rock – unswaying, unfaltering ... solid. But in that brief snapshot, seconds before his face creased into a smile at seeing me, I caught a glimpse of his mortality.

I had a good visit as my dad, despite being tired and breathless, was in high spirits. I, along with my mum and Joel, was quite certain that he would be home in a few days. It was Emma's birthday and my dad told me to go out and have some fun.

'Come and see me again tomorrow,' he said, as I got up to leave. It was then, when walking away, that I turned to my dad and let rip with those three little words. What prompted me to say them then, as opposed to at any other point in my life, I don't know, but whatever I was feeling in that moment, I'm certain, my dad was feeling it too, which is why he said them back.

Emma and I partied that night, drank a bit, danced, had a good time. I didn't think about my dad. When I'd called the ward earlier that evening, they had told me he'd eaten a good dinner, and so I was positive he was on the mend. And anyway, I knew I would be visiting him again in the morning.

I was fast asleep when my phone rang at 3 a.m. – so fast asleep that I didn't even hear it ring, which is why Emma was woken up by Joel ringing her phone.

Emma woke me up.

'Dad's on life support,' Joel said down the phone. 'You need to get down here now.'

I remember Emma shaking me awake, but my brain was unable to engage. It seemed to be slipping on the gears. I must have taken in what Joel said though, as I got up and, without saying a word, went to brush my teeth. When I came back into the bedroom, Emma was fully dressed.

'Where are you going?' I asked.

'I'm coming with you.'

'You don't need to,' I said. The truth was, I didn't want Emma to come with me. If she was by my side, it implied that this was serious, as if we were expecting the worst, when we weren't. This was just routine. My dad was going to pull through. I tried to put Emma off, but she was determined.

'I just want to be with you,' she said. 'I can stay in the car.'

I don't remember getting to the hospital. We must have sped in the car down the A13 because that was the route. When we arrived, Emma came in with me, as I knew she would, and we made our way to the high-dependency unit. My dad was there, attached to a whole bunch of wires, unconscious on his life-support machine. The room smelt of disinfectant and stale coffee from the vending machine outside, and the lights flickered like some kind of spooky horror film in the dawning light. I couldn't bring myself to look at him. It wasn't my dad lying here. My dad was at home, sitting in front of the TV, where he always was.

We were directed to the visitors' room. My mum was sitting in a chair, head down, hands clasped together, while my brother paced back and forth in silence. Seeing us arrive, my mum's eyes filled with tears, worry lines etched around her mouth.

'Pray that he won't die,' she cried.

'He won't die, Mum,' I said. Offering supportive words to my mum was my default, but also I believed what I said.

'Just pray,' Mum said. I joined my brother walking back and forth across the tiled floor, praying inside my head. Emma took care of my mum, which, to this day, I am truly grateful for. Sitting next to her in the chair, she stroked her back and prayed alongside her. I could never have done that. All I could do was withdraw into myself. I didn't have anything else to give.

There was another family in the visitors' room alongside us; a Muslim family. As we prayed to the God we knew and loved, they prayed to the God pivotal to them in their lives. Despite our different religions, world-views, and walks of life, our sentiments matched. We were all looking for support in our time of dire need. I seem to recall that even then, I was able to acknowledge the beauty of faith.

My mum's prayers were not the same as mine. Hers came from a place of desperation: 'Please, God, don't let him die. Make him better. I beg of you, God. Let him live.'

My brother's prayers ... well, I don't know what he was praying for as he, like me, does not open up easily. My faith as I paced the visitors' room floor that night hinged on hope, which lay in the fact that the God I loved and had worshipped all my life would perform a miracle and cure my dad. I was certain he would do this for me. How could he not? He had the power. He could make things right. And if ever I needed him to give me something – anything – it was now. That was why I believed 100 per cent that my dad would pull through.

This was not the first time I had prayed for a miracle. I had done it one time before, when I was in Year 8, around thirteen years old. I was outside playing football when a massive storm tore through the playground. The whole school was called inside, but me and my friends ignored the whistle and carried on playing because at that age, we were invincible.

I remember seeing the lightning strike and feeling it hit the ground as it took me with it, knocking me off my feet. The sensation was unworldly. It felt for a short moment as if all of time stood still. I stood back up, dazed and disorientated, and noticed all of my friends were doing the same – except Izzy. Izzy was lying motionless on the ground. Stumbling over, we found him unconscious, body torn, with burns melting the skin beneath his shirt.

The teacher came running out and began CPR, pressing his chest and breathing into his mouth, trying to resuscitate him, but he didn't come round. The ambulance showed up and we were all led into school as he was carried away.

Izzy was in intensive care for months. At first, I prayed every single day for God to perform a miracle and make him better: 'Come on, God. It's within your capability to do this.'

After a few weeks, with no improvement, I began to get despondent. Until that point in my life, I had never doubted my faith. I had always had full confidence that in my hour of need, God would be there for me.

But he was nowhere to be seen. How could that be?

He could clearly hear my prayers, so why was he not responding?

During that period of waiting for Izzy to recover I was as close to walking away from God as I have ever been.

I couldn't do it though. I needed God, because I needed the hope that God brings to our hearts. I decided to give God one last try and began praying with all my might for that miracle to occur.

This time, God listened, worked his wonder, and my friend Izzy made a full recovery.

That is why I believed in miracles.

If God could do it for Izzy, he could do it for my dad, no doubt about it.

So it was for a repeat miracle that I prayed that night, as the machines beeped and the hours passed in the high-dependency ward.

My dad would get through this.

My certainty was still fully intact when the doctor arrived at 6.45 a.m. and told us he was going to turn my dad's life support off. *It's okay*, I thought. *He'll breathe without it. God's got this sorted.*

Gathered around my dad's bedside, we said our goodbyes, but I still didn't believe it.

At 7 a.m. my dad left this earth for good and all hope dissolved.

Where was God? Why was he not there for me?

My mum fainted and had to be taken to a bed to lie down. Her heart was broken. My mum and dad had embarked on their life journey together; they were in it as one. Every thought, plan, decision had been shared between them. My parents had spent more years of their lives together than apart.

My mum did not want to carry on alone.

As I told you, I had not expected my dad to die. Even in the minutes leading up to his death, I had been convinced he would live. I blamed my numbness on my complete lack of preparedness.

My dad had died and any second now it was going to hit me.

Any minute ...

Any hour ...

Nothing came.

Just two weeks before my dad died, Emma had asked me what, if faced with a tough situation, I would need from her in order to feel better. She was attempting then, when life was on an even keel, to tap into some deeply embedded font of emotion. I had never got round to giving her an answer.

As Emma saw to looking after my mum, I kicked into autopilot, texting friends to impart the news and to offer them the opportunity to come to the hospital to pay their respects.

One hour later, after my mum had regained her composure, we left Queen Elizabeth Hospital, a place that less than a week before had hardly featured in my life, but would now hold a poignant place forever in my memory.

We were back at my mum's house from the hospital by 8.30 a.m. At 11 a.m., the mourning began, and when I say *mourning*, I don't mean hushed tones and neighbours posting sympathy cards through the letter box. No. I mean mourning Ghanaian style and by Ghanaian style, I mean *big*. To Ghanaians, bar the wailing and tears, there is very little distinction between mourning a loss and the classic house party.

Death provides an opportunity to dress up, gather crate

loads of drink, and arrive on the doorstep of the mourning family home in large groups for an extended visit that consists of talking, crying, and praying.

My mum, Joel, and me were ready for the onslaught – we'd been to mourning occasions before – but Emma was blown away.

'Will your mum be okay with all this?' she whispered as the doorbell rang continuously and hordes of friends and family streamed in, filling the garden shed with enough sustenance to last us through to winter.

It was just what my mum needed. This was not a time for her to be left alone. She needed the people, the love, and the warmth, and the house crammed full, because very soon it was going to feel very big and very empty.

That day, sixty people came to pay their respects. What I was not expecting was quite how tough I would find it all. As I told you before, inside the four walls of my home, we followed the traditions and customs of Ghana, it was the world I inhabited. Yet suddenly, everything that I had once classed as *familiar* was alien. So many people, so loud, so little room to move around.

Each new arrival brought another set of distressed faces: 'What happened, Isaac?'

Over and again, I had to repeat the same series of events. 'He started feeling ill last Thursday …'

This would be followed by a round of wailing 'Charlie's gone. Where's Vivian? Vivian, Vivian, I can't believe it. Charlie's gone.'

It was wearing. I realized a few hours in that all I wanted was to be left alone to process the enormity of what had occurred in the space of my own head, but this was just the beginning. Mourning Ghanaian style lasts for a long time.

For the whole week following my dad's death, there were

never less than twenty people in the house. I grew concerned at the emotional toll the house guests must be taking on my mum, as it was she who bore the brunt of everybody else's anguish. She cried continuously, for days on end.

'She must need some respite from her tears,' I said to Emma.

'Or maybe letting go brings her a sense of relief,' Emma replied. With her open nature, she had really got to grips with the whole outpouring of grief.

If Emma was targeting this comment in my direction, it was lost on me. I was too wrapped up in my own misery to understand the impact of my actions – or lack of actions – on other people. Emma was completely in touch and at ease with her emotions and fully able to impart how she was feeling. It was very hard for her to comprehend quite how hampered I was.

What neither Emma nor I could possibly have realized so early on in this journey of grief was quite how sustained the long haul would be. At this point in time, we were barely an inch across the starting line.

For the next six weeks, any of the peace and space I craved was on hold as there was the funeral to arrange. The limbo period was this long as many of my dad's relatives were coming from Ghana and it took time to issue visas.

As the eldest son, all of the funeral management fell to me. My role in the family had never been defined as 'second-in-command', but then again, none of us had expected my dad, the self-assigned head of the household, to leave us so soon.

It's funny how we all adopt certain positions within the family. Although Joel was happy to help and wanted to be involved, I didn't want to put too much pressure on him.

It never crossed our minds that it would be anyone else but me in charge. I needed to be in control, and so to be honest, I would instantly have dismissed any other option anyway. Perhaps, deep down, I valued being practical, busy, and focused, as it prevented me from having to face the darkness that was lurking inside my mind.

At my mum's request, the funeral had to be big.

'He worked hard all his life. We're not going to bury him like a mouse.'

If my dad could have had a hand in the arrangements, his priority would have been for us to save money. He had conserved money all his life, so why blow the whole lot at the end?

But my dad had no say and we wanted to do him proud, pay him the respect that he was due. Anyway, my dad never said 'no' to a party, and so that is what he would get.

A lot of my comfort in the run-up came from my church community in Bermondsey, south-east London. This was when I realized that going to church was more than just ticking a box on Sunday, as people rallied round, bought us food (yeah, more food!), took me out, called me up to check on me, and contributed money towards the funeral. I felt very privileged to be a part of this extended Christian family.

Six weeks is a long time to wait for a funeral. On the surface, I thought I was holding everything together pretty well, but to my nearest and dearest – namely, Emma and my two closest friends, Nick and Joe – there were cracks. I'll get to those down the line, but for now, let me tell you about the moment I cried … and kept crying.

I've already told you about how me and crying had something of a strained relationship – this whole form of emotional release did not come easy. I wish it did and I used to envy people who could just turn on the tap, but for me crying was a big deal. Before my dad died, there were occasions when Emma would say to me, 'You need to be more in touch with your emotions,' and I would try and force myself to cry, to prove to Emma that I could. But it never happened. When you have been led to believe that crying is wrong, it's not easy to backtrack, even for someone you love.

Yes, there'd been the odd tear, but the first time I properly cried – full-blown wept –following my dad's death is worthy of its own paragraph.

We were a few days into the extended mourning period and my house was jammed full of bereaved partygoers. I was in the kitchen opening a bottle when two of my dad's best friends came over. After we did a bit of chatting one of them said: 'We loved your dad, Isaac. You know that, don't you?'

'Yeah, course.'

'And we know it's going to be really tough for you all from now on,' the other said.

'I know.'

'While we can never replace your dad, we want you to know that we're here for you. We came to this country together and we're going to stick by you. If there's anything you need, anytime, day or night, you just let us know.'

'Thank you,' I said. 'I will.'

As we drifted apart, I felt a surge of emotion swelling inside my chest. My dad must have really meant something for them to make such a heartfelt offer. I opened the back door and went into the garden, holding my mouth, to keep the sobs from busting out. I had barely got past the shed before the tears surged thick and fast. I tried brushing them away. It wasn't the time nor the place, but they kept on coming.

Walking into the shed, I busied myself, working through the crates of donated food, taking deep breaths. I knew people would understand if they saw me crying – of course they would; I had just lost my dad – but it mattered more for me that they should see me strong. It's what my dad would have wanted and, most probably, have expected.

That said, for the first time since my dad died, I went straight to sleep that night and didn't wake till morning. For the short spell the release lasted, it felt like a great weight had been lifted off my shoulders.

On the work front, I shut up shop in the long wait for my dad's funeral. There was not any creative space in my brain and anyway, there was too much administrative bureaucracy to work through. However, there was one gig that I did accept, because I knew my dad would not have wanted me to miss it – the Allo Mate Live event that I run annually in Shoreditch.

I put it on for younger artists to showcase their talents and then I perform at the end of the night. I dedicated the performance to my dad as a personal tribute, with a photograph of him up on the stage behind me (picture 3). It was really important to me that I did that, and I am so pleased I got to put his memory into the public domain.

My dad's funeral took place at St Chad's Church in Chadwell Heath and 400 people attended; that was 400 family, friends, church community, neighbours, and colleagues. I always knew that my dad was a *good 'un*, but there is a chance that I was biased. Hearing his friends and colleagues talk about him though, I knew that what I felt was bang on.

No one spoke empty words; every snippet, memory,

and character reference came attached to an anecdote or example. My dad was remembered as someone anyone of those 400 people could call on for help, any time of the day or night. For many, he was known as 'the driver', because he was always happy to drive anyone to where they needed to be. One of his colleagues told the story of how, every single working day for a year, my dad had driven out of his way to collect him at 5.40 a.m. from his front doorstep, to take him to work as a favour to the colleague, who didn't have a car. What particularly cemented the image of my dad as a legend in my head was that, despite this friend constantly offering, my dad never accepted one penny towards travel expenses or petrol. He did it because he liked helping others.

My dad was laid-back and easy going, got on with everyone, and had never had any reason to argue or fight. Best of all, though, my dad was remembered for his laugh. As I told you before, he never said much, but he laughed his way through life.

He loved music and so it was essential to me that I got that right. We had some gospel musicians accompanying a gospel singer, along with fellow MOBO award-winning saxophonist YolanDa Brown. Both my brother and me delivered speeches about my dad. It was tough and the tears rolled when I spoke, but I got through it.

We owed it to my dad to show everyone who he was, all that he'd achieved, and everything that he meant to each of us.

After my speech, my dad's friends came up to me and said, 'Well done, Isaac, you were strong, you were brave.' I know that if I had broken down during my speech, they would have said something more along the lines of, 'Never mind. You tried your best.' I am very relieved I was strong and brave.

What does that say about me and my conditioning?

We followed the hearse to Rippleside Cemetery in Barking, which was to be my dad's final resting place. My mum stayed in the car as he was lowered into the ground, too fragile to follow through with the final goodbye.

It was with the natural sense of relief that follows any long period of waiting that afterwards we kicked back at the wake my dad deserved, by hiring the same DJ we'd had for his fortieth birthday party. It went on for several hours and he would have loved every moment of it (picture 4).

For the weeks leading up to the funeral, every smile and laugh had been tinged with guilt that it was somehow disrespectful to show humour so soon after the death of a loved one. Personally, I don't agree with that mindset as there were so many memories of my dad that I wanted to laugh out loud at, but as the eldest son, I'd felt the need to set some kind of an example.

What was great about the party afterwards was that following the dignified farewell, it was acceptable to joke, because that was exactly what my dad would have expected of us, and what is more, he would have joined in 100 per cent.

5. WHO AM I?

In June 2017, one month before my dad died, I turned twenty-eight. I was a fully grown, happily married, working man (picture 5). I had stuck to the straight and narrow pretty sensibly, knew my own mind and was, on the whole, in tune with what made me tick.

And then my dad died and my whole life turned upside down.

I had never been a big drinker. At university, when most were downing pints and playing drunk Jenga, I would be off at a music gig, performing or in the audience, or at the house I shared with my housemates, writing lyrics and compiling playlists. I had fun. Yeah, I loved university, enjoyed my Business course, got on well with all my friends, but I wasn't what comes to mind when you think of a 'typical student'.

When the nightly drinking crept up on me, I was taken by surprise, as I rarely drank at home. For the first week after my dad died, I slept in my old bedroom at Chadwell Heath, keeping an eye on my mum and helping my brother manage the constant stream of visitors. By week two, however, I was keen to get back to sleeping at my flat alongside Emma, as I craved peace, quiet, and solitude. Every day, I went over to my mum's house in the morning and every evening, I came back home knackered from talking and listening all day long. Emma was at the flat waiting for me and I realize now that she was worried that I wasn't taking any time for myself. She most probably said as much, but after removing my shoes, landing heavily on the sofa, and burying my head in a cushion, my auditory receptors were down, as my ears were overloaded with words and I couldn't process anything new.

At first, it was one drink before bed just to break the silence – a small glass of Amaretto Disaronno with a cube of ice. It warmed my belly and because I was in high-tension mode, its effect went some of the way towards soothing me. Most importantly, and the bit I didn't face up to, is that it also worked as a veneer, shielding me from the rage and shock lingering in the shallows of my mind.

Over the weeks, the single shots multiplied into doubles, then a double and a single, sometimes a double plus a double. I needed the double dose to help me sleep. I needed a double and a single, plus a double, to keep me asleep for the duration of the night. I tricked myself into believing that sleep was essential for knitting my emotional wound, therefore the drink that enabled it was my friend.

The mind is a powerful force, especially when we are at our most vulnerable. We can tell ourselves anything if it makes us feel better – and we believe it. With my logical brain I was able to rationalize my drinking so that it made perfect sense.

I caught sight of Emma watching me one night, several weeks into my drinking. I had moved onto the Jameson's whiskey and was pouring my second double. She was on the outer edges of my peripheral vision and because she thought I couldn't see her, she didn't make any attempt to look away. I didn't say anything and she kept quiet too.

What was there to say?

Over the course of the weeks, we had not spoken much. I had been busy at my mum's house during the day, and in the evening I didn't have any mental energy left for anything except to drink and sleep.

That night, like all the other nights before, Emma went to bed ahead of me and I sat alone on the sofa, waiting for the drink to take effect. Up until then the barrier I had built between myself and the world around had felt okay, like the right thing to do for self-preservation. That night, however, for the first time in a long time, I gained a glimmer of perspective: my drinking was getting out of control and I needed to rein myself in.

I owed it to my dad,

I owed it to Emma.

I owed it to myself.

But I wasn't sure I could do it.

I had become reliant on my drink to sleep at night. Was I ready to face the alternative? Was I ready to take the hard path when the easy path was laid out before me? I tried reflecting on any words of support that my dad would have said right then.

'Stop the drinking, Isaac.'

'Why?'

'Because.'

'Because it has hijacked my sleep, Dad? Because it's forcing me to shy away from reality? Because I like it too much?'

'Because I say so, Isaac.'

'Fine.'

Picking up the glass, I went into the kitchen, poured the liquor down the sink, and watched as the cold tap water chased it away. I put the lid on the bottle, put the bottle in

the cupboard, shut the cupboard door, and went to bed.
End of.

Three months after my dad died and a short while after I quit my daily drinking routine, I received an email inviting me to support the singer songwriter, Matt Redman, on tour, in the USA. This was a great opportunity for me, but I was not sure I was up for it. Was I strong enough to spend three weeks away? Was my mum strong enough for me to leave?

I had scrapped the album I was due to release before my dad died because it was so far out of kilter with where I had suddenly found myself, By that I mean that it no longer felt true to who I was. So, without the album to promote, I decided that touring the USA would be a good move and, more importantly, a necessary break from my new reality.

My flight landed at LAX and I bedded down at Matt's pool house on Newport Beach to sleep off the jetlag before hitting the tour bus and 'taking America' … well, some of its big cities. The tour bus was great because I had a bunk at the back and the team we were travelling with were all cool people (picture 6). The bus driver was from Nashville, ex-military, gun-toting, and pretty crazy. I'll give you an example of how crazy: on our first meeting, he showed me how to fire a Taser.

Over 5,000 miles away from London, it was easy to forget about my home life and the all-consuming death and grief. There were around fifteen or so travelling on the tour bus, so I was able to tap into other people's worries, jokes, and life events, all of which were refreshingly worlds away from my own. At other times, I just sat back and watched the vast distances and sweeping horizons roll by.

We travelled to Los Angeles, Nashville, and Atlanta, which was cool because one of the venue owners took us to the Mercedes Benz Stadium, where I got to see my first Major League Soccer match. We also visited Fayetteville, in North Carolina. This location resonated with me, as it is here that one of my favourite rappers, J Cole, lived. I went for a walk on Forest Hills Drive, an old address of his, and the name he gave to his third album: *2014 Forest Hills Drive* (picture 7).

The most noteworthy part of the trip, though, was in Las Vegas, as our concert took place the night after sixty-four-year-old Stephen Paddock, the Las Vegas shooter, killed 59 and wounded around 413 on his Las Vegas Strip murder spree. The whole city was out that night, and we were there lighting candles, singing, praying together in one mass memorial. I treasure being a part of that and the mood and atmosphere is something I will never forget, as my subsequent Instagram post reveals.

Allo Las Vegas Such an emotional place to have the last tour date but it was a privilege to witness such hope and light in what has been some very dark moments. After the show tonight we went outside to light some candles and sing some songs. Special moments. (Instagram, 5 October 2017)

On my last night in LA before I was due to fly back home, I bought a notebook and went down to the beach. This was the first time I had been in complete solitude since my dad died. Sitting on the white, soft sand, looking out at the Pacific Ocean as the waves rolled back and forth, I was struck by how big the world is and how small we are; how every single one of our lives matters, but only to the tiny number of hearts we touch.

I opened my notebook, took hold of my pen, and

unleashed the words that had been locked inside my head since my world stood still on 18 July. A song titled 'Carry On'. was the result. It was as if the sentiments were all lined up, waiting to be set free, as it took me no time to write.

On the 18th of July 2017
3 a.m. I was asleep when my wifey intervened …

… A yo, my daddy lived a good life,
And even though we had good times,
I couldn't even say goodbye.

I closed my notebook, lay back on my hands, and looked up at the star-studded sky. This was the moment it struck me that nothing in my life was ever going to be the same again. I had crossed a bridge between the old me and the new, and I was at the point of no return.

I didn't yet know quite what that meant. It was more of a feeling than a fact, but in the short space of time between losing my dad and that moment, I'd lost touch with who I was and everything I believed myself to be. What I suppose I'm trying to say is that it felt as if my life had been built on sand and I was struggling to find my grip.

The distinction between the old and new me made, I now had to travel back home and figure out 'My Life, Part II'. I was not looking forward to taking on board the new Isaac because my heart didn't feel hospitable enough to welcome a stranger. All of my life I had fallen back on the personality traits that defined me – laid-back, logical, a man of faith – but that wasn't me. Not any more. I wasn't laid-back, happy to let life roll by; I was bewildered, knocked sideways, out of control. Irrationality had skewed all logic and the trust I put in my faith to light the way had been overtaken by fear.

Queuing up to board the plane the next day, I flicked through the pages of my passport. It was in the name of Isaac Charles Borquaye and that was definitely my face staring back in the photo, but all similarities between me and that man ended there.

Exiting Arrivals at the airport, I scanned the waiting sea of faces for a glimpse of my dad, like I always did when arriving home. It was an agonizing undertaking, but I challenged myself to do it.

Why?

Who does that?

I needed to do it.

It had been four months and apart from the brief bawl in my mum's shed, I was yet to slice through the numbness that had taken up residence the day my dad left this world.

This was the one of the first times my dad had not been there to greet me on my arrival home. If the enormity of his loss did not touch me now, when was it going to?

I primed myself for the breakdown, the tears, pain, sorrow.

It didn't happen.

The Uber driver pinged my phone to inform me that he was outside waiting in a black SUV.

'Good trip?' he asked as I climbed into the back seat.

'Yeah,' I said, positioning the headphone on my ears.

'Where have you been?'

'Huh?'

'Been anywhere hot?'

'Er ...'

Why did it matter where I'd been? Why was he asking? Why was my dad not here to ask me? I felt my forehead prickle with sweat and my fists curl. Did he not realize that the only reason I was in his car was because my dad was dead? I was struck with the overwhelming need to punch out the tinted windows, livid all of a sudden at the world for letting my dad, the most significant man in my life, leave so quietly.

How could life go on so seamlessly, day in day out, when mine was stuck fast, frozen to the spot, unclear as to which way to turn?

Was I really expecting tears and sadness? How meek and mild. What I needed was rage; rage at life for robbing me and getting away with it; rage at the world for moving on; rage at my dad for succumbing; at my mum for allowing my dad to succumb; at God for taking him so soon; at myself for not being there for my dad – and most of all, at the Uber driver, for filling the empty void with mindless chat.

'Been rubbish weather here,' the driver said.

Was he actually trying to rile me?

Slumping into my seat, I pulled the hood low over my head and shut myself down. At least if I was numb I was safe to have around. Raging was a whole different ball game. Right then, I had no idea how I was going to react to anything thrown my way, so it was better all round if the world just left me alone.

My best friend, Nick, wasn't having any of that though. I saw him a few days after I got back.

'This ain't really like you,' he said to me.

I was surprised at him saying that, because I thought that publicly I was masking how I felt, holding it all inside. That's best mates for you though, isn't it? They know you through and through.

Nick's been one of my best mates for as long as I can remember. We've shared both heart warming and heart-breaking moments together. He was standing next to me as I opened my AS level results and found out I got two

Es and two Us (LOL). I was sitting next to him when he got a phone call informing him that one of his close friends had just been shot dead. I celebrated with him the day he signed his major record deal, and he celebrated with me the day I got married. That said, it didn't mean I was going to make it easy for him.

'What do you mean it ain't really like me?' I asked.

'You're quite withdrawn.'

'I'm fine.'

'No, you're not.'

We might be best mates but on the emotional front, me and Nick are diametrically opposite. Opening up comes naturally to him. He learnt to express himself as a child, thanks to his dad showing him how to tune into his inner soul. I don't think I am an unemotional person by nature; I think the reason I come across as unemotional is because my parents never really listened to what I had to say. They didn't encourage me to talk. When it came to communication, what mattered to them was that I listen, keep my thoughts to myself, and heed their words.

Nick's parents actively encouraged his input. His views were important. That is why Nick is adept at telling it like it is – sometimes he tells it too much like it is, lacking any kind of a filter.

'So,' Nick said, 'what's going on?'

It was now barely five months after my dad had died and everyone was expecting me to have adjusted back to normal, got over it, moved on. This was the advice I was receiving loud and clear from the church community, the people who craved the positivity that our faith provided. In this instance, however, the upbeat outlook was not working for me: I needed to bathe in my grief, let it enfold me. I was not yet ready to step out of it and face the world unarmed.

That I was still feeling like this, however, weighed heavily on me. Should I still feel lost and confused nearly half a year on? Was it right to feel so angry and alone, and out of sorts?

The reason I was withdrawn is because I didn't trust my rage and because I was unable to process my feelings – rage was pretty much all I had to work with.

I wanted to open up to Nick because he loved me unconditionally and I knew that he could take it. He was emotionally robust and had only my interests at heart. He is a hard taskmaster and he wasn't going to let me walk away without giving him something to work with. I told him that I was confused, like I was sinking. He suggested that I talk to a professional, someone who could help me work myself out. I appreciated the advice, but wasn't ready to go down a road like that. He suggested we meet up more regularly than our standard every couple of weeks so that I could get stuff off my chest if I needed to. That sounded like a better plan and so I agreed to do that.

With my other best friend, Joe, who I have known since I was in Year 7, the friendship was a bit more light-hearted. I love comedy and Joe makes me laugh. He was a good tonic at this time, as he didn't demand I dig deep. With Joe, I could lighten up, let the anger seep away.

If you want to get an idea of how my friendship worked with Joe, check out this Instagram post I wrote in March 2018, which says it all:

Since year 7, me and my boy Joe have Been Hustlin'.
We were always looking for some kinda dodgy deal
to get involved with. One time when we were 15,
we were walking to my Mum's house and Joe saw
an old Fiat Punto for sale. He goes to me 'Oi, come
we buy that car.' Me being the law abiding citizen I

was, I replied 'Yeah come then.' The car was £500.
Joe was playing for West Ham youth team so he
was getting a little £. I was broke but I did have 2
phones for some reason. One of them was a Nokia
95 fresh out the box. Next day we went to go see
the guys selling the car and Joe had his £250. The
guy looked at me for the other half of the p's and I
said I ain't got no money my g but this Nokia phone
is too sick, you need it in your life. He chuckled, took
the phone and handed over the car keys. My gift of
the gab had me feeling like the black Del Boy. Only
problem was we couldn't drive away because neither
of us could drive. Brotherhood (and Sisterhood) is
really important. You need good friends to make
mistakes with, to learn with, to grow with. We've gone
from sitting in detentions together and buying cars
without driving licences to professional careers and
comparing mortgages. Most importantly, through
our experiences we've learnt about what's really
important in life and we're able to help people around
us not make the same mistakes we did.
(Instagram, 7 March 2018)

All the while I was figuring out my own pain, I had my mum's
pain to deal with. She, like me, struggled with the societal
view that grief ought to last a finite amount of time and that
we Borquayes should be back on our feet by now.

'You'll be fine' was a comment we heard over and again.

How did anyone know? It was only when the three of us
were together – my mum, Joel, and me – that we could let
down our guard and wallow in our shared misery, except
that, for Mum, the misery was too big for either my brother
or me to bear. It got to the stage where calls were coming in

night and day from my mum, wanting me to fill the gaping hole that my dad had left behind, even though both of us knew that anything I was able to offer was never going to make up for what she had lost.

I accepted every call because I knew how much she was hurting inside but after a while, it began to take its toll.

As children, we grow up knowing that our parents are going to die … most likely before we die. We accept this as a fact of life. We also accept that the role of the parent is to bring up the kids and care for them, knowing that one day, a long way down the line, the children will return the love and support back the other way.

That's how it should be at least.

What I was not expecting was for my dad to die halfway through his life, in the middle years, when my brother and I were not yet ready to shoulder the care of our parents, and they were not yet ready to need it.

When my dad died, it seemed to me, for a while at least, that my mum aged by twenty years. She was only fifty-four, but she went from being independent to dependent, from care-provider to needy, and from strong to helpless practically overnight. The problem with this sudden change was that I was not yet ready to adapt to the shift in the parent–child dynamic. I needed my mum to be tough and in control, and visionary, because that was all I'd ever known her to be. I didn't want my dad's death to alter my life out of all recognition. There needed to be something of the old world to hold on to.

As a consequence of my inability to fulfil all that my mum required of me, I added guilt to the mix, trying desperately to maintain a semblance of normal life that I put out for the world to see, while promising to be there for the new version of my mum.

Turned out, I was ineffectual on all fronts.

I have always been prone to bursts of guilt. It comes from straddling two worlds, where I was always trying to please everyone. Until this point in my life, my guilt had centred on feelings of inadequacy at never being able to live up to the expectations of my parents; that I was somehow letting them down, while at the same time, not wanting to diss the world I had been born into. This guilt was as much a part of me as my arms and legs. It was guilt and I knew no different.

After my dad died, though, I was bowled over by a whole new kind of guilt; guilt that showed up like an unwanted house guest, ate all the food, and refused to budge. I didn't want it hanging around, but I had no idea how to move it on. My mum used to call me several times a day wanting to talk, needing advice, and at times, draining me of the sliver of energy I was relying on to get me through.

I would go and see her and declutter her house, sort out the unopened bills and cards that were piling up in the hallway that she was too overwhelmed to open. All the while, I felt guilty because I could not make my mum's life better by bringing my dad back; guilty that I could never be the man my mum needed in her life; guilty that I was not doing enough for my mum; at the same time, feeling guilty that I was doing too much, which prevented her from moving on.

My guilt became so unbearable that it affected every part of my life. Instead of feeling naturally sad at the loss of my dad and upset that I would never see him again, I felt guilty that I had never made the time for him when he was alive, that I had put my work ahead of my dad.

It's true. The proof of my distraction was laid bare on my phone. My dad would text me, and because I needed space for my music, I used to delete various texts including his. If I had had any idea of what lay ahead, I would have treasured every single one of those messages. Instead, I only have a few left.

These make me laugh because they sum up my dad and technology (picture 8). And this, written just over a month before he died (picture 9). That was it. (Also, I realized I need to charge my phone battery more often.)

My guilt about my dad left me feeling frustrated, resentful, and overwhelmed by feelings of helplessness, which had a knock-on effect on my own sense of worth. I was angry at myself on a daily basis for being unable to reach back into the past and make things better and withdrew from those around me as I struggled to place myself in a world where I didn't belong.

I was asked recently, if I could turn the clock back to any time in my life, when would it be? My answer to this was that I would turn the clock back to my *Secret World* tour in 2015, when I performed with Michelle Williams from Destiny's Child at the O2 Academy in Islington (picture 10).

If I had the chance to go back in time and do this amazing concert again, I would make sure I brought my dad along to see it. One of my greatest regrets and guilt factors regarding my dad was that he never got to see me perform at a sell-out show. In Round Two, I would not take 'no' for an answer; I would force my dad to be there.

He would say: 'Sorry, son, but I've gotta work,' because he was like that, but I would go the extra mile. I would want him to experience the vibe, and the joy, and the audience interaction and, of course, for him to see me up on stage. He never got to see that big time, and I never made it happen for him. Why didn't I make the effort?

My dad was probably the most shy, private person I

have known, always happy to remain in the shadows. An example of how private he was is the time he came to my DVD recording at the Hackney Empire. Afterwards, when speaking to the cameraman, he never let on that he was my dad. He made out that he was just a regular punter because he didn't want to draw attention to himself. That was what he was like: wanting nothing from no one, at peace with himself and who he was.

If I could turn back that clock though, I would drag him to every show and take him around the world with me on all my tours.

My nearest and dearest – namely, Emma, Nick, and Joe – tried to get me to release myself from this guilt and disproportionate sense of responsibility. They assured me that my dad had been happy and content and suggested I put boundaries in place so I could take better care of myself, but I didn't listen. I was of the belief that no one in the world knew the enormity of what I was going through and so nobody was capable of helping me. I had to go through this alone. My dad's death was entirely on my shoulders. I was driving the recovery truck solo.

Even Nick, who rarely offered any slack, struggled to smash through my misplaced sense of self-importance. I was playing out every family role – dad, mum, big brother, and son – and the only way any of us were going to get through this was with me in front controlling the helm.

Was I really that essential?

No.

But I am a man of action. I need to fix things and seek solutions. When it comes to fixing things I think in black and white. Grey unsettles me. That is why I had such a problem dealing with my grief. Grief is grey. There is no quick-fix solution, no timetable for grief, no right answers. It hits you in unexpected ways and when you least expect it.

The truth is, I was scared. I could never have admitted that at the time. Grief caused my life to become wild and uncontrollable. All of the systems I had in place that sustained me and kept me secure, went out the back door and left me floundering. The only way I thought I could get through my grief was by taking charge. That is why I allowed my mum to become dependent. That is why I refused help or support from any of the people capable of making a difference.

I was going to fight this grief alone because I was strong. 'Leave it to me.'

6. WHAT NEXT?

I used to fear being found out, and my impostor syndrome was through the roof. My worst nightmare was someone saying or doing something that would embarrass me, show me up, so I would end up revealing who I really was. It was why having the gap in my teeth used to upset me so much, as it opened me up to being victimized. Just like someone saying something funny at my expense and me not being able to come back quick enough with a witty retort.

I was equally worried about saying something which might upset someone else, or come out wrong, which is why I was the King of Avoidance. It was easier to steer clear than to take any risks. I suppose I wasn't all that different from my dad after all – anything for a peaceful life.

For the first twenty-seven years of my life, my overriding preoccupation was the image I put across to other people. Was I likeable? Was I gangster? Was my music all right? Did I look good? Did I have the right clothes, shoes, car to impress?

I've told you already about the disappointment I felt when I eventually got the trainers I wanted. You might have thought I'd have learnt from this, that I would dismiss consumerism for the superficial high it gave. But I didn't, because fast-forward a couple of years and I was fixated on buying a BMW 1 Series. That was all I needed to make my life complete.

One year later, I was sold one by my best mate, Joe. Before you ask, no, it did not complete my life. In fact, the ease with which I was able to come by the so-called 'car of my dreams' diminished any sense of status I had in driving it.

I didn't keep that car for long. There was no point. As far as I was concerned, it had passed its sell-by date long before it came into my possession. I just needed to get it to prove that I could.

For a while after my dad died, I was torn between the self-conscious old me, desperate to maintain the strong Isaac image – looking good; sounding good; portraying the perfect image; the man holding it all together; keeping the family safe and sound – and my role as new Isaac, who just wanted to let it go.

Only one avenue provided me with the release that I craved and that was my music. In those days, it would take me a while to get my lyrics down. I needed time to process my thoughts. It could be a couple of hours before anything bubbled up to the surface, then I had to work to get them sounding just how I wanted them to sound. I now know that this is because back then, half the time, I was not writing the lyrics for me; I was writing them for other people. I was people-pleasing, trying to second-guess what my fans wanted to hear and that did not always serve me well.

In 2013, I released my album *Odd1Out*. I was really excited with this work and had great hopes for it being the sick masterpiece that would elevate me above the glass ceiling and up to the next level. The song I had the highest hopes for was 'Free'. It had a cool sample from a big dance song and I was so sure of it doing well that I expanded my team and invested in areas that I hadn't invested in before, like PR and a radio team. I paid a radio-plugger £1,000 to promote 'Free' for me, which was a lot of money for an independent artist back then.

At first, he was keen, telling me he would get my song onto Radio 1, but as soon as the dough hit his account, he went quiet and all talk of Radio 1 evaporated. In the end, 'Free' only got one play and that was on something random like Cardiff FM. After this I felt really dejected, as I had invested all that money and never seen any payback. I lost my trust in the music industry and in myself, and I felt anything but free.

Free

You're free
To do what you want to do.
You've got to live your life
And do what you want to do.
You're Free

I now know that what was happening was that I was trying so hard to put out what I thought people *wanted* to hear, without ever stopping to ask myself what *I* wanted to say, what was in *my* heart. This whole album release was a bad time for me. I remember voices in my head saying, 'You need to get yourself a proper job, Isaac. This music hobby is not working for you. Wise up, get a mortgage, start making tracks in a *respectable manner*'.

I took to my room, where I used to just sit alone with more thoughts going around and around my head: *You're not good enough*; *You're never going to make anything of your life; Why have you chosen such an untried music path?*

I started comparing myself to other people, which made me feel even worse.

Advice to anyone reading this: *Never compare.*

I never told anyone how I was feeling, and I went through a dark time with my music.

In the end, *Odd1Out* did pretty well. I became the first rapper to top the official Christian and gospel charts, and I was number 4 in the Official Urban Chart. But it was not an easy ride to get to that point as I didn't fit into the mainstream box because I was too much a man of faith, and I didn't fit into the Christian box as my music was too commercial and not traditional enough for Christians. So, topping those charts was a big statement for me.

Fast-forward to when my dad died, and in those deepest, darkest days of grief, my lyrics flowed, and they were lyrics unlike anything I had ever written before. My inspiration didn't come from other people, the streets, or from the image people had of me; it came from deep within and the words were intimate and meaningful. It was as if my aching soul was bypassing my reasoning brain and exposing my innermost, as yet unexplored, feelings.

As I mentioned before, I'd been about to release a new album when my dad died. I had been working on it for a while and was super happy with it. In my heart of hearts, I was certain people were going to like it.

I had written it with the aim of exciting my fans, imparting hope and solidarity in a shared love of God. It was joyful and playful, the equivalent of Saturday morning adrenalin TV with songs entitled 'Happy Days' and 'Top of the World'.

This was going to be my seventh album release after *The Narrow Road,* and I was in a good place as the *Secret*

World album had done really well (picture 11). My music was maturing naturally, along with my own maturity and life experience, but even with the world not being in the best state, in terms of crime and violence, I still trusted that God was looking out for us.

My decision to abandon my upcoming album is a clear example of how much my dad's death affected me and made me see life in a completely different way.

It only took a few months for me to change my outlook so completely that I hardly recognized the Isaac who had innocently penned those lyrics. That was old Isaac, propagator of positivity: 'Life is good. God is good. Be yourself.'

Even if I didn't believe in what I was writing, it was what I had been conditioned to think other people wanted to hear. The truth is, it was all I knew to write about, and it had been a success.

Up until this point, 'Nothing but the Blood' on the *Secret World* album had been my biggest hit. I dropped it just before Easter Sunday 2015 and it received over one million streams and two million YouTube views. With this track, I had adapted an old hymn to bring it up to speed with the modern day, which was quite revolutionary at the time.

A million. Mad ting. Thanks everyone! When we wrote this modern version of a classic hymn we had no idea we'd hear so many amazing stories of people connecting with it. Definitely one of my proudest moments (Instagram, 2 December 2017)

A lot of people liked it because they already knew it as a hymn, but for other people it somehow connected spiritually *and* musically.

Nothing but the Blood

Yo, me and Adam, man, we've really got to have words.
I'm sorry, brother, but I heard you made it all worse.
I'm stuck, I don't know what works.
I know it ain't all your fault.
You're just as flawed as me.
And plus, I know what it's like when I let Satan talk
    to me.
And yo, I've read all these books.
And I've read all these verses.
So why when I progress, do I get caught reversing?
I'm trying to keep it moving.
Just trying to find your grace.
But I just feel like in my life, I've made so many
    mistakes.

What can wash away my sin?
Nothing but the blood of Jesus.
What can make me whole again?
Nothing but the blood of Jesus.

They think I'm crazy.
And they don't understand where I've been lately.
I've been battling myself, but can he save me?
I put my faith upon that shelf and yeah, it changed me.
You could tell that I've been lazy.
It's the world that I was craving.
But then I had a dream.
He said that life ain't even always what it seems.
Every test is a lesson,
Every lesson is a blessing,
If you choose to see the message.

And so I'm here.
And I'm still standing by his grace.
It disappeared.
And all my failures,
All my shame, now I see clear.
And that's because no other name has brought
    me near,
And I can't wait to see his face.
I'm pressing on.
All my mistakes, they are erased.
And now I'm strong.
It's like the judge has closed the case.
I can move on.
And yeah, I've moved from place to place,
But now I found where I belong.

Secret World and 'Nothing but the Blood' were all me, but in the past. With my dad's death, it was as if someone had lifted the shiny trainer to reveal the dog crap underneath.

In discovering my own vulnerability, I was suddenly able to appreciate it in other people. It was all very well writing songs that were up in the clouds and airy-fairy, but how did that speak to the kids who were on the receiving end of bullies at school on Monday morning?

Death brought me to a whole new level of understanding. Through my lyrics, I was able to open up in a way that I had never opened up before. It was like I had been granted permission to communicate more deeply, because now, I too had experienced unfathomable pain.

What was amazing about my letting the album go and writing lyrics for my next was that, for the first time since my dad had died, I was allowing myself to grieve. Okay, so I wasn't grieving outwardly – no one in my life knew I was loosening up as I still wasn't strong enough to face up to people eye to eye – but I was finding the vocabulary I needed to release myself.

Looking back, I realize now how helpful it would have been if I had opened up to those closest to me sooner. I do believe the process might have been less painful and passed more painlessly, but because I was certain that what I was feeling was totally unlike what anyone grieving had ever felt before, I just didn't feel comfortable doing this.

I now know that everything I felt was normal, because when it comes to grief, the boundaries of 'normal' are wide, or to put it another way, nobody experiences grief in the same way. It is as unique and ordinary to each of us as our own DNA, and so everything added together = normal.

This post gives you an idea of where I was in my head a couple of months after my dad died.

Can anything good come out of difficult situations? The cliché would say yes but I'm still trying to work it out. What I do know is that while I'd give anything to have my Dad back, i've learnt a lot in the last few months and i take the stuff he taught me a lot more seriously now. I'm not completely out of my dark place yet but I'm starting to get used to my new normal. I think that's okay though. When you make the kind of music i make, you're expected to be positive 24/7 and to have it all worked out. This album isn't quite that but I hope it provides the right balance of honesty and hope. Because there's always hope. Hands Are Made for Working is out now. (Instagram, 18 May 2018)

I recorded *Hands are Made for Working* in the final months of 2017 and early 2018 and had literally had no idea how it was going to go down. I named it that because it was what my dad always used to say to my brother and me when we were growing up. And if anyone was a hard grafter, it had been my dad.

Carry On

I remember back day when you told me, 'Tidy your
    room.'
You was popping to shop, but you said you'd be back
    soon.

As soon as you left, feet up, I was watching the cartoons.
Time of my life till you got back 'bout half past two.
Blood, I ran to my room started scrambling.
You was coming up the stairs, feet stamping.
Burst through the door. I saw your face: you weren't
    ramping.
I started making up excuses. I was rambling.

Then you did your cheeky little grin, then you bust
    out laughing,
Felt like you want to be angry, but you just couldn't
    help it.
Then you walked over to my bed, sat down and
    called me over.
I thought I was about to get the belt or something,
    but you just sat me in your lap.
You took my hand and put it in the air.
Then you said, 'Son, never be lazy. Hands are made
    for working.'

Even though he was entitled to twenty-five days' holiday a year, my dad never took his full quota. How mad is that? They were there on a plate, but if there was any work to be done, my dad would do it. He viewed work in the same way that I view work – as an escape; a place to put your focus on the job that needs doing and dispel all other thoughts of life.

The lyrics for my *Hands are Made for Working* album were fresh data delivered direct from my heart. I wrote them from inside a vacuum, consisting only of me and my grief working side by side.

I wrote this Instagram post on 13 November 2017, four months after my dad died:

> I'm putting out some new music next week. Haven't put anything out in a while so I'm looking forward to sharing some again. In the last few months I've learnt that life doesn't always go according to plan and it's really tested my faith.
>
> Previously I've always felt the pressure to have it all worked out and for my life to be in a pretty good place before I can share my art. You know like the 'I used to struggle with this but now life's great' kinda vibe.
>
> Recently I've learnt that there's beauty in the struggles that life brings and there's strength in vulnerability and honesty. So now it's more like 'Sometimes I still struggle, life isn't great again yet, but I'm trusting one day it'll get better.' Come along on the journey if you fancy it. My new single #Everyday is released on November 24th. P.s I read this the other day. It's sick.
>
> Why am I almost never satisfied with what I have, but always wanting more? Why does absence

make the heart grow fonder? Why is the pursuit of achievement often more enjoyable than the achievement itself? Why does loss, hard times, and suffering often produce the best character qualities in us while comfort, ease, and triumph often produce the worst?

The more you desire something, the more you will be satisfied when you get it. It is through mourning that we know the joy of comfort. Emptiness makes us seek and wanting makes us ask.

Sometimes the tougher times help mould us into the people we need to be.

(Instagram, 13 November 2017)

I first met my producer, Jimmy James, back in 2007, on Myspace.com (picture 12). He had just produced *Dublit* by Sammy G, which was an album that I liked, and so I sought him out, on his farm in Coleshill, Warwickshire, to produce some music for me. Since then we have worked together on all my albums and he has become a good friend. We have sort of followed the same life path of marriage and kids. He is godfather to my son, and I am godfather to his son ... that kind of thing.

The first hint that perhaps I had produced something meaningful was when I recorded 'Carry On' in the studio with Jimmy James. It was the first time I had let the song loose, and I really did not know how he was going to react.

I looked up after singing the last line and saw that he had tears in his eyes, which took me by surprise. He hadn't even pressed the button to stop recording. Jimmy James is someone who always holds it together. I didn't even know he had a sentimental bone in his body. His grandmother had just died so I think that was why he felt the rawness of the lyrics so intensely.

'That's sick,' he said.

'Really?'

'Yeah.'

'Cool.'

I was pleased that Jimmy James liked the songs, but even if he hadn't, I would still have classed the songs on that album as my best work ever. They were 100 per cent honest and 100 per cent authentic, I believed in every word I wrote and the album pinpointed exactly where I was at that moment in my life.

With all my previous album releases, I had been worried and fearful that people wouldn't like what I was putting out, that I would have an *Odd1Out*, Round Two. With *Hands are Made for Working*, my mind didn't even wander into the realms of fear. It was as if, since my dad died, I had conquered fear. Either that or all of my more mundane fears had been put into perspective. Nothing was as bad as losing my dad, so what was there to worry about?

I was no longer concerned about being defined by record sales or success. The only worry I did have was that the music might be so hard-hitting it would bring people down. I played a couple of tracks to some of my friends to get their take. If they had told me the tracks were too depressing, I wouldn't have included them on the album, but they listened and suggested that I go ahead.

I released 'Everyday' first. It had been several months since anyone had heard any music from me, so there was quite a bit of anticipation. Anyone expecting happy, celebratory Guvna though, was in for a shock.

Everyday

I gotta get it together, it's been a mad time.
Ain't been the same since my Dad died.
I been anti, yeah, I got struggles too.
Caught off guard, heart cut in two.
I'm in the car with his CD, running tunes.
He told me he loved me, I love him too.
I don't really know what to do.
My heart broke that day in the hospital.
God puts to use what he puts us through,
But it's hard sometimes tryna trust the route.
I'm a man of the house, tryna hold it down.
My brain's a mess when I stroll around.
I wanna try my best, but I don't know how.
Dad's in heaven, I wanna make him proud.
I wanna raise the roof, I wanna shake the ground.
But I can't forget that he ain't around.
I'm skipping sleep cos my thoughts are loud,
But I'm digging deep, tryna sort it out.

The reaction was totally unexpected. 'Everyday' was my best-selling song to date. That was a surprise. I was actually expecting to lose a few of my fans due to its painful content.
Instead, it went the other way.

I released *Hands are Made for Working* a few months later and it reached number two in the iTunes UK Hip-Hop Album Chart, so I guess it hit a nerve. Seemed that whatever I was feeling in those dark days, other people were feeling too, in their thousands. It was realizing that – more than any amount of success or excitement for the album – that blew me away. All that pain. How had I not realized it before? Seeing the reaction to 'Everyday' and to a couple of the other songs I put out before the album went on sale was what inspired me to write 'Broken', which I recorded, featuring singer–songwriter, Elle Limebear.

Broken

Everybody is broken
Everybody breaks

I was on Forest Hills Drive,
Listening to Forest Hills Drive.
The Uber driver played Love Yourz,
Then he told me catch vibes.
Nobody's life is better
And Nobody's life is worse.
Gotta see life as a blessing.
I can't see life as a curse
Everybody's got their path,
The road is never even.
Everything we ever loved
Is found in broken pieces.
It's mad – just look at my past – but
Touch my pulse, I'm still breathing.
Yeah, my bones are still healing,
They're healing

Wrote this out of principle.
I thought I was invincible, a saviour to myself. It never
    helped.
I nearly risked it all.
Didn't make no time for my loved ones.
They wanted more.

I put my dad in my diary, but then had to take that tour.
Promised that I changed my ways.
I can't talk right now, going on stage.
I know I've been away,
But I'll make more time when I get space.
I thought I needed the space.
Now I'm at home, just me on my ones.
Just me on my ones. What have I done?

We're all in need of saving.
There's loads of different places
We choose to put our faith in.
All this time I'm wasting.
Everyone's got a drug and mine was alcohol.
That only made me angry found my inner Al Capone.
I tried to hide my feelings, but the truth you never hide.
So I went to see a counsellor for my bucket load, my
    pride.
I'm not ashamed to visit, we're all broken, just admit it.
Jesus, only you can save me ...

Since the early release of some of the songs, I had engaged with my fans in a way that I had never done before. It's amazing how, when you open up, people open up in return. Until that point, if people had asked me how I was doing, I would always say, 'Fine'. And that was it.

'Fine' is a safe answer. You can't go anywhere with 'Fine'. These lyrics though were me opening up and saying, 'Actually, I'm not fine. I'm hurting.'

On reflection, you could say that when I wrote that album, I wanted it to be a blueprint of how to deal with difficult situations, to let people know that it's okay to cry. When life is bad, you think that the bad is there to stay. I had no idea how in need of a blueprint people were. It was as if everything I said resonated far and wide.

One of my favourite parts of performing is doing the signings after the show. That's when I sit at a table in the venue lobby and get to meet the people who relate to my music, who follow me and support me. It's an amazing opportunity to connect with the people I think of as my 'extended family' and get a sense of who they are and why they enjoy my music. These signings are invariably high-adrenalin: happy people coming up, high-fiving, praising God, praising me, praising the beauty of life.

Hands are Made for Working (*HAMFW*) is a record of my own personal journey through grief. The earlier songs on that particular album centre on the raw shock and bewilderment I felt straightaway when my dad died, but in the later songs, I can start to see signs of a way forward, light at the end of the tunnel.

With the release of *HAMFW*, these signings took on a whole new character. No small talk, no fist punches, we were straight to the heart. People were coming up to me saying, 'Guvna, I'm hurting inside'; 'Guvna, my mum died, and your words spoke to me'; 'Guvna, thank you for opening up'.

I was blown away.

Really?

That much of an impact?

And it has been that way ever since.

I thank God every day for this new insight and depth.

By the time I reached the last track on *Hands are Made for Working*, I was beginning to find my hope. 'Summer in the Streets' was inspired by me finding a CD in my dad's car. I had gone out to his car a couple of days after he died to grab some of his possessions. There was a CD in there that he had got his DJ friend to make for him. He loved this CD; it had disco and funk and '80s songs on it. I put it in my car to listen to and fell in love with it instantly for its sentimental value. There was this one song on the CD by Carrie Lucas called 'Summer in the Streets', recorded in 1984, which was my dad's favourite song.

So, I got Jimmy James to work on the beat and I added some lyrics. That song bought me so much joy as I knew, with my Christian faith, that one day, I would see my dad again up in heaven and when I did, we would play that song on repeat.

Hands are Made for Working touched a lot of hearts. I only toured London, Birmingham, and Manchester with it, but in all those places, I came across people suffering every bit as much as me, not only from the loss of someone important to them, but also from the loss of a job, an opportunity, or direction. Way more people were hurting than I ever could have imagined, and it made me think: maybe this is my purpose – to connect with people on a deep emotional level. This is an Instagram post I wrote in response to the feedback I received from the album:

> It's exactly six months since *Hands are Made for Working* was released. We didn't really have any expectations for it but @its_jimmyjames & I felt that it was just important to put out something honest and true. The numbers are cool but the best thing has been reading all your stories. Knowing the album connected in such a deep way and is therapy for a lot of people is a special feeling. Even on a personal level i've have seen continuous examples of God's love, generosity, peace, grace and favour.
> (Instagram, 19 November 2018)

Summer in the Streets

Summer in the streets,
Sounds so sweet.
You'll be there with me,
The way it used to be.
Summer in the streets,
Sounds so sweet.
You'll be there with me,
The way it used to be

God, when you're ready, come take me away.
I ain't really scared of death no more.
2017 wasn't good for my brain.
I can't really deal with the stress no more.
What's next though? Wanna pull up to your gates,
    wanna head home.
Can't take another day, I wanna rest loads.
Cos my Dad went, then Daisy went 5 months later.
Best know I was really close to the edge.
Suicidal thoughts, coulda jumped off a ledge.
But Mum wouldn't know how to cope. Lil bro wouldn't
    learn all the ropes, and Emma would be all alone
Can't lie still, call his phone, hope he picks up.
Got his photos all on my insta.
Gotta be strong, be a better me, I gotta stop with this
    negative energy.
You worked too hard for the legacy. Now all the
    advice that you gave me is making sense.
Cos that baton that you had, I gotta take it next and
    do something.
I promise that I won't trip, Cool runnings.
Tears when I wrote this, I do love him.

Can't lose focus. Tryna finish my race and do you
    proud, till I see you again in new summers.

I put all my hope in the saviour.
So I'm praying that I'll see Dad later.
When i get my mansion up there, i hope you're my
    next door neighbour.
Might bring a couple pads, play Sega.
First console you bought me was mega drive.
FIFA 98 and Crash Bandicoot, those were the days.
But there'll be better times.

The following is one of the many messages I received
after the release of *Hands are Made for Working,* and was
accompanied by a drawing (picture 13):

Since my dad passed away, I've struggled to come to
terms with it and why it had to happen. 29 years and
I've never seen my dad sick and the one time I do he
doesn't get better was hard for me to get my head
around. But thanks to my cousin @anton_ferdinand5
for introducing me to @guvnab I was introduced to
an album that has helped me to deal with my loss
because it was made in the time that he was dealing
with the same thing. Yesterday I got to see him play
that album live and it was music therapy and I know
it will help me in my journey going forward it was a
pleasure to meet him as well and have a chat and for
the love and time he has given me over the last few
months. So to say thank you I drew a picture of him
and his late dad for the opportunity that he has given
me to heal through his music.

I'm just going to go off here, and tell you about my dad's Adidas trainers because this is a happy memory, alongside that of 'Summer in the Streets'. I mention the trainers in the lyrics of 'Carry On', as this memory means so much to me:

Thinking bout all of the memories we had
Like when I first got sponsored by Adidas we were the
    same size
So I used to give you all the trainers I didn't like
Your favourite were the Stan Smiths

My dad loved those Adidas trainers. I say we were the same size, but my feet were a size eleven and he was more like a size ten, but that didn't bother him. They were well-made shoes and that's why he wore them. He had no interest in what brand they were. He would have worn anything on his feet so long as they were comfortable. Just like he didn't mind that the Honda he drove around was a rust bucket that embarrassed my mum – the engine was good and that was all that mattered to him. I used to laugh at my dad in those trainers, a fifty-five-year-old man wearing a twenty-one-year-old's shoes.

But he didn't care.

7. EMMA AND ME

I first met Emma through a friend who basically set us up. I was single and not really looking for anyone at the time. At university, I had been quite promiscuous. I guess it was my way of rebelling against my restrictive upbringing and struggling to get to grips with being outside of my comfort zone. Following that period of my life, I wanted to focus on being a better me so I had no interest in anything long-term and marriage was definitely not on the cards. My parents' marriage, though not without friction, had always appeared solid as a rock, but I had seen too many unfulfilled marriages, whereby couples had gone in happy and ended up unhappy, only staying together because it was the *right* thing to do. This put me off wanting to risk falling into the same trap.

Our mutual friend Ben Lindsay produced a photo of Emma, announcing that he knew someone he thought I would get on really well with.

'Sure,' I said. 'I'm happy to meet her.'

We married in 2015.

Happy birthday to the girl that always lets me finish her food. Glad I pulled her for a chat a few years ago to see where her head was at. I grafted and then we cracked on, and it's been a pleasure seeing her grow. Cos she's Em, and she's real, and she's loyal. (Instagram, 23 July 2018)

Anyone who enters into marriage convinced that it will consist of one long, eternal honeymoon needs to reassess their life plans. Marriages take work, even when you love each other with all your heart. There are curveballs that life rolls your way with the express purpose of tripping you up.

When my dad died, I can see, looking back, that I lost my way in my marriage. Even prior to his dying, I was not an easy person to live with, as I have never been someone who needs other people. I am self-sufficient and independent, able to rationalize myself out of any emotional dead end.

Emma, like my friend Nick, is completely in touch with her emotions and never short of the vocabulary needed to express them. Where I run on logic, she runs on feelings. As a consequence, we both come at the same situation from a completely different angle.

With my dad's death, I closed down, shut myself off, internalized my grief, as my default was to handle my dad's passing alone. These actions were completely incompatible with the way Emma functioned, meaning that for quite some time we were strangers to one another.

Emma and I have spoken about this a lot in the years since 2017 – and she's given me a few peeks into her diary from around this time, so I think I understand some of what was going on in her head. Emma, my wife and soul mate, on seeing me suffering, wanted to help and comfort me. Her approach was to hold me close, protect me from my grief. It's a natural reaction when you see someone you love in pain.

For me though, this level of physical intimacy risked tipping the scales on my sensory overload that was already running at maximum revs. Any more input and my fragile state of mind would have imploded.

Of course, me being me, I couldn't tell her that, because I never would have found the words to explain it; so instead, it appeared as if I was pushing her away.

I know that it was a really confusing time for Emma as I was completely unpredictable and gave out a whole load of mixed messages. Sometimes I was withdrawn, other times angry, other times in a frenzied state, as I tried to take back control of my life. We both know now that this is quite 'normal' – that word again – but at the time, it was really upsetting for both of us.

This is what Emma wrote in her diary on 27 October 2017:

> I feel like I go round in circles, trying, feeling rejected,
> getting upset with Isaac for not showing me love,
> feeling like I should give up, and then trying again.
> But the problem is that I am not involving God. I think
> I can find a solution to a problem that is so much
> bigger than me. But I can't! God can!
> I need to step aside and let God take the lead and
> TRUST him.

The way Emma handled it was to back off. I don't know how she knew to do this, but it was the right thing to do, even though it went against her compassionate nature. I think that she was worried that by backing off it would look like she didn't care, as if she was moving on and leaving me behind, but it never came across like that as I always knew she had my back.

She had this sort of system in place that was to ask me,

once a day, if there was anything that she could do for me. I didn't register that she was consistently asking me this, as my head was all over the place. I always answered 'no', most probably forgot to thank her sometimes, but she persisted, because that was her way of showing me that she was hanging in there.

I'm not sure how it is for you, but I remember growing up, watching my parents behave towards one another in a particular way and thinking, *that is never going to be me*. I intended to reinvent the wheel and take my own untried, untested path. Then I got married and pretty quickly, I slipped into the role of my dad. I adopted his passive nature. I could never understand how he could devote so much of his life to that L-shaped sofa. Now, I get it. I love working, but I could just as easily bed down for forty years living in the here and now.

That same passive nature came to the fore with my grief. All the while I thought I was running the show, managing the fallout of death, but I was, in reality, doing nothing practical to help myself. I had taken a seat in the Observation Gallery and was sitting back, watching life tick by.

I justified this approach by telling myself that the only way I could possibly see to fix this would be to bring my dad back, and because that was beyond my powers, there was nothing I could do.

Emma has always been way more proactive than me and what I didn't realize was that all the while she was backing off and giving me space, she was quietly putting in measures that would put me back on the road.

A bit more from Emma's diary (27 October 2017) – as I told you, she is proactive.

I'm going to write a list of things I can do for Isaac and
    pick one:
Try and keep the house clean
Encourage him every day to build him up
Organize his merchandise
Pray for him every day
Call his mum often
Do the food shopping
Look for houses
Review our finances so he doesn't have to
Be the one to initiate date night
Initiate prayer time
Give him bible verses to read
Cook meals he likes.

So much of the problem with death and dying is that until it breaks down the door and invites itself in, you never think it will happen to you, and so you don't put any coping mechanisms in place, especially when, as was the case with my dad, it takes you completely unawares. One day you wake up and your dad is at home, a smile on his face; the next day, he is dead and gone forever. Nothing can prepare you for the shock.

That was why Emma took a crash course, courtesy of Google, on what to expect with grief. It was her way of managing events.

I'd like to say that I took on board some of her research, but I didn't. I spurned it. I made my dad's death *my* problem, and didn't let anyone else in. It was really hard for Emma. It was as if she was suffering her own version of bereavement by losing me to my grief. I had changed almost out of recognition and she had no way of knowing if I was ever going to return to how I used to be. The truth is, I don't know how she stayed so strong. Before my dad died, we had been a partnership; we had committed to one another that we would 'do' life together, but suddenly she was on her own. I am sure there were times when she needed me, but I was so wrapped up in my own misery that I never even noticed her crying.

Emma's diary entry, 27 October 2017:

I feel so lost. I don't feel like I have a clue how to help him. I always (before this) felt like I hadn't ever had the chance to get to know him as well as he knows me because he's not as vocal with what he wants/needs/ feels...it's overwhelmingly difficult. I feel like every time I try and help him I'm doing it all <u>MY</u> way and it's not actually helpful. He needs me to just 'leave him be,' but surely that can't be it. That can't be <u>all</u> I'm meant to do. It pains me – it breaks me – to see him struggling but not be able to do anything to help him.

I think he is keeping me at arm's length as he doesn't want me to be overwhelmed with the weight of it too and then I'll be another thing for him to have to worry about. I don't know how to prove he can trust me in this. Maybe I will never be able to prove it during this situation.

What I really could have done with when I was sinking deep into my guilt and confusion would have been someone taking me to one side and saying, 'Isaac, it's normal to feel angry when someone dies. It's normal to feel sad, lonely, guilty, and out of sorts, and like a stranger, and confused, and as if you are on a road to nowhere.'

Had someone told me that, I would have relaxed into where I was. I would have said, 'Okay, this is weird. I don't like what I'm feeling, but it's all part of a normal process. It's a human reaction to loss.'

But nobody said this to me. Correction – I never *heard* anyone say it to me. Chances are they did, but for several months during that period of mourning and grief, I closed my ears off to all around.

Anyone looking to carve their own path in life steers clear of the word 'normal'. We strive to be different, to rewrite history, stand out, and make our mark. When it comes to our health or our grief, though, 'normal' is good, because normal means that we are wired to feel like this and to react to death and bereavement in a particular way. Most importantly, it means that we have the inbuilt tools to get through.

Elephants are amazing at grief. They get it. Elephants are known for experiencing many of the same emotions as humans because they live for a similar number of years. This means they develop similar close bonds with family members. When an elephant dies, the rest of the herd moves into grief mode: their ears droop, they hang their heads, they are silent, and they go through a whole burial ritual. That's because they understand intuitively that grief is necessary in order to heal. I wish I'd been that in tune.

Other creatures grieve too: gorillas and songbirds. Dolphins slow down the speed of their swimming to escort a mother carrying her dead calf, and giraffes hold vigils. So yeah, feeling out of sorts when somebody dies, is *normal*. What is hard for humans is to accept it as normal, because while we have a mourning phase and a funeral ritual, even post-death anniversary rituals, we don't have a *grieving* ritual. For the grieving, we are left on our own to figure it out, which is why it turns our whole world upside down. We have no idea how long it is going to last and what impact it is going to have on the way we function.

Other side effects kicked in as well: I developed a real chip on my shoulder which meant that because of losing my dad, all sympathy and empathy for anyone else's problems, mishaps, or worries went out of the window.

My thinking was that, unless the other person's problem was on the same scale as my problem, it didn't count:

You've had a bad day? At least your dad hasn't died.

Split up with your girlfriend? Yeah, but you've still got a dad.

Had your phone stolen? What about me? I had my dad stolen.

It got to the stage where my sense of proportion was totally off the scale. If I had not had such a firm network of good, loving friends, I am certain people would have ditched me as I was not good company.

With that chip on my shoulder, I stopped caring about other people's stories, which was not like me. I love listening to stories and hearing what makes the world around me tick.

People don't always realize this about me. They think, *Oh he's on stage the whole time. He must be bursting with confidence.*

The reality is that talking about myself and spending hours reflecting on 'me' makes me uncomfortable.

In the depth of my grief, though, I only had ears for one story – and that was my own.

What I also found myself doing was adopting a victim mentality. I found out from Emma not that long ago that it got so bad she began a Google search: *Is my husband grieving or could he just be really annoying?*

Yeah, I had slipped into some really bad domestic habits and Emma was rightfully worried that once a person gets into particular marriage patterns, these are hard to shake off. Basically, I turned into the sloth that had typified me in my youth. I stopped doing my share of the cleaning, I stopped tidying up after myself and clearing my plate after eating.

The concern for Emma was how much of this was Isaac grieving and how much of this was Isaac taking her for a ride.

I'm not going to lie: I reckon it was around 50:50. I'm not proud, but there was a part of me thinking, *Hmmm, I'm onto a good thing here.*

Sorry, babe.

I'm pleased that Emma is the person that she is, because she started putting her foot down assertively. She didn't do this harshly, but with grace, suggesting I clean the bathroom and then following it up:

'Have you cleaned the bathroom?'

'Can't remember if I suggested you clean the bathroom.'

'Oh yeah, you said you were going to clean the bathroom.'

What I discovered after a few days was that getting back into the groove with my domestic routine was good for my mind. Starting jobs and finishing them gave me some of the control that I craved and, at least for the moments when I was engaged, it went towards clearing the constant fog that blurred my mind.

Just to give you an idea of how detached Emma and I had become from each other, Emma bought a book called *Good Grief* by Granger E. Westberg (1913–1999), a Lutheran priest and professor, all about – as the title suggests – *doing grief right*. But she didn't give it to me because she was unsure how I would react. My anger and distance had got so bad that my own wife could no longer gauge how I would respond to her love and support. She hid the book in the wardrobe hoping that I might find it, but at the same time, a bit scared that if I did find it, I would accuse her of trying to analyse me, which I would have classified as interfering.

It was a perplexing time.

Eventually maybe six months after my dad died, we were chatting – just everyday chit-chat; nothing noteworthy. I don't remember how we got onto the subject of how I was feeling. I guess Emma steered the conversation in that direction in her subtle, super-intuitive way, hoping to eke something out of her tongue-tied husband. Anyway, I found myself giving her an analogy of how I was seeing the world: 'All around, there are people bringing sunshine into my life, but the sunshine can't break through the dark cloud that sits above my head accompanying me everywhere I go.'

Emma didn't say anything, which at the time I remember thinking was quite strange, as Emma *always* has something to say, particularly in response to me being in the rare position of baring my soul. I looked over at her and said, 'That's weird, isn't it? A dark cloud?'

'What's weird,' Emma said cautiously, 'is that I read that exact same description in a book.'

'What book?'

'A book about grief.'

'You've been reading about grief?'

I don't know why I was surprised, but I was. I suppose it never crossed my mind that grief was enough of a 'thing' for it to be put into a book, which now I think about it, was pretty naive. Of course, there are all sorts of books on grief. It is after all a completely normal phenomenon.

'It's just a small book.'

Emma got up, went over to the wardrobe, opened the door, and produced a paperback. She handed it to me.

'It's really thin,' I said.

'I didn't think you'd want to read anything longer than a pamphlet.'

She had a point – I'm not a big reader.

Emma opened the skinny little manual and read out the exact same analogy I had just given her.

One way to describe depression is to say it is much like a very dark day when the clouds have so blacked out the sun that everyone says, 'The sun isn't shining today.' We know the sun is shining, but it appears as if it is not.

'That's it!' I said. I couldn't believe it – it was as if she had read my mind word for word.

'This is what it says depression is like,' Emma said reading on.

Something seems to come between the person and his fellow men so that he feels a tremendous loneliness, an awful sense of isolation. And he can't seem to break through it.

'Sound familiar?' she asked.

It did. It felt not only familiar, but bang on.

We grow up hearing the word 'depressed' bandied around and it's just another label.

'What's wrong with him?'

'Oh, he's depressed.'

It's like when people say, 'He's annoyed', or 'She's having a bad day', we acknowledge it but let it go, with the general view that whatever the problem is today, it will be gone by tomorrow. It never struck me that depression could commandeer my mind and infiltrate all aspects of my life.

'Do you think you ought to see somebody to talk about it?' Emma asked quietly.

'I'll be fine,' I said. That answer was my default. I had no idea if I would be fine, because I had no idea what depression was, or what its impacts were, or how long it might last. I just needed some time to process this latest batch of intelligence.

What did feel good was to know that I was not the only one playing host to a dark cloud, and that it was 'normal' to correlate clouds with depression. I was at least on a level with the rest of the human race.

Depression though? Wasn't that like a backache? Something people talked about as painful and debilitating, but because there are no cuts or bruises or crutches or bandages, no one really cared?

Later that day when I had a bit of time alone, I sat down and read *Good Grief* from cover to cover. It is only eighty-two pages long, and I found I could relate to much of what Westberg was saying. I won't tell you too much about the book because it is better, if you want to read it, that you read it first-hand, but it covered a lot of what I was feeling, including depressed, guilty, and angry. I also googled 'depression', and 'counselling', and 'grief', and searched: *Do I have depression or am I just sad*? ... just in case it turned out I wasn't depressed at all, but was an impostor trespassing uninvited into mental-health territory.

Whichever way I looked at it though, it seemed that all roads led to black-cloud thinking and while there were ways in which I could help myself, I needed support in putting together a plan of action.

A couple of days later, Emma broached the subject of counselling for a second time and I agreed that perhaps it would help me get rid of the cloud and reclaim my life.

'So, Isaac, what brings you here today?'

This was the counsellor's first question. An obvious question for a counsellor to ask, but I wasn't prepared for it.

'Er, I dunno,' I said.

Silence.

More silence.

'My dad died.'

'Aha.'

'And ...'

'Yes.'

'And, I don't think I'm coping.'

Boom!

Despite agreeing to seek help, I was still not convinced deep down that it was the right course to take. I should have been able to sort stuff out myself. I didn't really have faith that anyone could help me, not anyone in flesh-and-blood form anyway. Whatever was going on at a spiritual level ... that was a whole different matter.

I suppose I was more deeply embedded than I realized in the Ghanaian belief system that if something is challenging to understand, then it must be part of a wider plan that is in the hands of the Almighty, and only the Almighty.

The counsellor was good: he knew the questions to ask, the body language to use, and when it was right to fill the gaps or leave them hanging. In fact, he was so good that less than twenty minutes into my forty-five-minute sitting, the emotion that had been bubbling just beneath the surface for weeks on end suddenly burst out, taking me completely by surprise.

'I'm sorry,' I said as the tears rolled out of my tear ducts and I wiped them off my cheek.

'That's okay,' the counsellor said.

Weirdly, it did feel okay. Here I was, a grown man, sitting across the room from another grown man and I was crying, and the man was not judging and telling me to be strong and manly and pull myself together. In fact, I would say, he was encouraging it.

I'm not going to say that words cascaded out of me, even though I like the word, 'cascade', because never in all my thirty years of life have words *cascaded* from me, but they did emerge in a pretty steady stream.

He got me talking about my dad, which felt good, although in terms of words, there was never a huge number of words to use in conversation about my dad. He was more of a positive presence, a strength, a force. It was not like I had a catalogue of my dad's greatest speeches or profound thoughts stored in my head, because this was my dad we were talking about, and he most probably never said much more than an instruction manual's worth of words in the course of his whole lifetime.

I still managed to talk about him though because, weirdly, in many ways, through death, he had become so much more alive to me than in life, which my counsellor told me wasn't actually weird. Often people become more alive to someone through death as they tend to take up all the bandwidth of their mind.

We touched on my depression. He told me that sometimes people did not experience grief as a transitory journey where, over time, the raw pain alleviated, and they learnt to adapt. Instead, some people were trapped by the pain and unable to progress. This was called 'complicated grief' and happened in the case of around ten to twenty per cent of bereaved people.

Grief: deep or intense sorrow or distress, esp. at the death of someone. (collinsdictionary.com)

Complicated Grief: Where grief becomes complicated people feel unable to bounce back. There is usually something about the experience that leaves the person who has been bereaved feeling stuck and in a struggle to cope with the emotional impact of their grieving. (Cruse.org.uk)

Complicated grief went some of the way towards explaining why, even though several months had passed, I was still feeling the pain of my dad's death with the same level of intensity that I had felt when it first happened. This is quite common when a death is sudden and unexpected, as you have no time to prepare. Some of the components of 'complicated grief' include anger towards the world in general, numbness that does not subside, a powerful sense of loneliness, and the feeling that life lacks any kind of meaning.

I felt all of these things in varying degrees, which was the reason for my depression. It was like I couldn't see a way to move forward.

I left the counsellor's that day with a series of weekly sessions booked up into the future and some pointers to implement into my daily life over the course of the upcoming week.

'You look different,' Emma said to me that same evening as we sat together on the sofa.

'Different how?' I asked.

'Sunnier.'

'Early days,' I said.

I wasn't yet ready to commit to this 'recovery programme'

100 per cent, not outwardly at least. Chances were that it would have no effect, and the last thing I wanted to do was disappoint those willing me on. But the truth is, I did feel better. The cloud was there, but knowing I had a release offered me a narrow sliver, and through that sliver, I was vaguely aware of a shard of sunlight maybe, possibly, perhaps just trying to shine through.

You

Life ain't fairy tales, that's real, but I love my girl.
Been down since 2012, I had a box-cut, no Jheri curls.
Know her very well, June 27th confetti fell.
That was in 2015, my dream, yeah, but lemme tell
It's not always roses and daffodils. You gotta know this.
If it's perfect, then it's showbiz.
That ain't us, if you notice
You left the washing out, I didn't fold it.
We argue, now we're joking.
Yeah, grown ting, you gotta know this, girl, it's you.

No girl can do it how you do.
I'm down for you and you're down for me, but what's
    new?
We ain't perfect, but it's worth it and that's cool,
Cause, girl, it's you.

Life ain't fairytales, that's real, but I love my girl.
Both had loved ones leave this world.
Both gave hugs when needed help (RIP).
I got you, you got me, even through hell.
You eyes see past my flaws and that's remarkable
    detail.

I apologize for the times I pretended I knew best,
Cause deep down, I'm still learning and deep down I
    feel blessed.
Baby mudda, you know I love you, when I'm out with
    you I gotta flex,
Cause babes you're peng, innit? Haha.
Girl, it's you.

Love that's patient, love that's kind,
Love that's true, love that tries.
We ain't perfect, but that's fine,
I got yours and you got mine.

8. STRIKING OUT

I might have jumped ahead a bit bringing my domesticated home life with Emma into this already, as there were a few more rocks and stones to cut my feet on before I got to the stage of sitting on that counsellor's couch, and they largely concerned God and me.

Something I haven't told you yet is what happened to me in the moments after my dad died. Don't get excited! It wasn't any great miracle or enlightenment, but more a sense of comfort. Sitting beside him in the immediate aftermath, I was hit with spiritual certainty about what lay behind God's thinking in taking my dad from us, and on some level, I saw God's plan in pure clarity. That happens with a bereavement, by the way: we look for messages and signs, and ways of making sense of what has occurred. Some people I have spoken to since tell me that they feel the presence of their loved ones in nature: butterflies suddenly appearing in the middle of winter; thunderstorms on an otherwise tranquil day ... that kind of thing. I never looked for messages, but I felt an instant sense of calm.

All his life, my dad's driving force had been his legacy. He needed the decisions he had taken in his life to bear fruit. My dad died in the same week that my brother graduated from Leeds University. He had seen his two sons educated to degree level, had been there when I collected my MOBO awards, and watched me succeed in my career. He had come to England with nothing and now owned three properties. He had had no chance to reap all that he had sown, but he had achieved everything he had originally travelled across the world to do. His life was complete. From where he came from that was quite some accomplishment.

I mentioned earlier on about my dad having had open-heart surgery when he was younger. I was eight at the time and too young to remember what happened vividly, but when going through some of his stuff after he had passed away, I came across an old hospital letter from the day he had surgery. The letter was a 'permission to operate' form. The surgery was so complicated that my mum had to sign a form confirming she was well aware that this was high-risk surgery and that he could die. Not ideal, but there was no other option – he needed surgery. The thing about this letter that knocked me for six was that it was dated 18 July 1997. That's right ... twenty years to the day. To. The. Day.

Could it be that his death was God's higher plan? That in 1997 God had spared my Dad's life because his work on earth wasn't yet complete? That he had been granted another twenty years to secure his own future, as well as his kids', and to see me and my brother graduate and start our dream careers?

We had thanked God for saving him twenty years earlier, so should we have trusted God in deciding to take him now? Seeing my dad lying there looking so peaceful, I was certain in that moment that this was the case.

But ... that was *then*.

As the weeks rolled by there were times when I struggled to believe these moments of comfort had happened at all.

It was like it had all evaporated, like scalding steam. So much of the anger I felt for the world around me was, if I am honest, directed at God. What right did God, in his almighty wisdom and power, have to take my dad away from me, from my mum, from all of those lives he'd touched? Why take the good and leave so much sorrow in the world? Why punish the faithful?

That I was even questioning God concerned me. It was like questioning the purpose of my feet to walk, or my eyes to see. He was essential to my whole being, but at the same time, he had performed an act so utterly mystifying that I was not sure how I could find it in me to forgive him. This led me to wondering whether I would even be able to love God again.

Can you love someone who has betrayed you?

It was around this juncture in my life, a few months after my dad died, that thoughts of suicide began to seep in.

You know by now that I'm an avoider of conflict – or a 'hedgehog', as I have since been called, as I prefer to roll up into a prickly ball than to scrap. In the same vein, whenever the going gets tough, I run. Most of the time I run towards work and bury my head in as much of it as possible, because when I'm performing or touring or writing, I don't have to think about anything else. I'm not particularly proud of this trait. I would like to think of myself as someone who faces adversity head on, but that's not me. The only other time I had really felt like running was in my first year at university when I hit rock bottom.

I had been in need of money to pay for my music and so made the rookie mistake of opening four student bank accounts at the same time, all of them offering an up-to-£1,500 overdraft limit.

I reckon you can guess what's coming next. Correct! I

maxed each one out, getting myself £6,000 in debt straight off the bat. Honestly, I didn't have much of a clue about managing money. I've already told you that when I got £4,500 from the launch gig of *The Narrow Road* I blew it in a month. Money back then was such a rarity.

For a lot of my life, my parents lived hand-to-mouth: they would earn the money and spend all of it straight away on food, bills, and rent. As a result, they never gave me much of an education regarding how to save. They were both aspirational people who lived just beyond their means. If they could afford a £200,000 mortgage, they would push themselves and go for a £250,000 mortgage, then struggle to meet the monthly payments. I respect them for thinking big because it was inspiring to see first-hand how they pushed themselves, but without a doubt, they made life hard for themselves.

Thinking about it, the best place to learn about managing money should be in school, but schools never teach useful stuff like banking, mortgages, tax; they teach you how to find the square root of an Adidas trainer store, but not how to spend your money wisely when you're in there. Who's used a protractor since school? Definitely not me.

Anyway, when the letters started arriving on my doorstep fining me big time for my debt, I went into avoidance mode, burying my head and ignoring the letters, so the debt and the fines grew until I was so out of my depth I could see no way of ever finding the funds to pay the money back.

The shame I felt about the mess I had got myself into prevented me from being able to tell anyone.

I had good, supportive friends, but chose to isolate myself, as I couldn't handle the harsh judgement that I was sure people would throw my way. I saw my inability to get a grip as a sign of personal weakness.

1. Me meeting the great Kirk Franklin, 13 June 2015

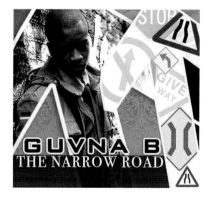

2. *The Narrow Road*, album cover

3. Me dedicating a song to my dad at Allo Mate Live 2017

4. The fam, with my wife, Emma

5. In Greece on holiday with Emma: carefree, just before my dad died

6. Touring USA, 2017

7. Forest Hills Drive, 2017

8. Text conversation with Dad, 24 October 2016

9. Text conversation with Dad, 13 June 2017

10. O2 Academy Islington: one of the venues for my *Secret World* tour

11. Secret World at Number One in the Charts

12. Me and my producer Jimmy James

13. A drawing of me and my dad by a fan

14. Em and Me

15. Daisy's Christmas card December 2017

16. One of my best friends passed away 2 years ago today. Been thinking about her a lot throughout the day and then I just saw this rainbow. Felt like it was God reminding me that he's got her. (Instagram, 19 December 2019)

17. Me and my dad

18. Me and Daisy Morgan

19. Fisko and me

20. Me with Sheila, an unexpected fan

21. Vivian Maier photo: the inspiration for the *Everywhere + Nowhere* album cover

22. Man is happy

Thinking thoughts of this nature led me to feeling useless and hopeless. With that level of shame, I deceived myself into thinking that the worst thing I could do was open up. I already told you that I used to be someone who minded deeply about how I was judged. I still do, to a degree, but back then it was an immense part of how I conducted myself. If people had found out how much debt I had accrued, they would have lost all respect for me, and when you're a black kid from an inner-city estate trying to find your way in life, respect is everything. You're born into a life where you're constantly undervalued and seen as *less than*, so the fight to be somebody is a real one.

That was where I was when I decided the only option I had was to run – and by *run*, I mean end it. A £6,000 debt plus interest, with letters coming to my door every week, was a lot to deal with mentally, especially for a guy like me, who didn't come from money.

So, yeah, I contemplated suicide, weighed up a few methods, but my intention never extended much beyond a fifty per cent likelihood of actually doing it, as concern always kicked in for the person who would end up finding my body. I couldn't bring myself to put any of my loved ones through that. It was one thing to ruin my life, but what right did I have to ruin someone else's?

So, it was fear that prevented me from dwelling too long on death. Instead, I decided to commit myself to the next best thing, which was figuring out a plan of action.

That was the hardest part: admitting the error of my ways to my friends. It took me a long time to summon up the courage. I expected people to tut, turn away, look me up and down, and say, 'Never expected that of you, bro'. But that never happened. What I learnt at that point in my life, a precursor I suppose for what was to come, was that when you open your heart and reveal your inner soul, the results are nearly always positive. Sharing my problems with my friends liberated me and simplified what, in my head, had become a problem of off-the-scale complexity.

I'm sure you've heard the saying that 'a problem shared is a problem halved'. Well, don't ignore it, because it's true. There was nothing any of my friends could do to help me pay off my debts, but just having them listen non-judgementally put my worries into perspective.

Nick got his dad, Gordon, to sit me down and teach me how to manage my money, which was enlightening to say the least. I had no idea how little I knew.

From then on, I began saving like mad. Every penny I earned from my shows and music sales I put into paying back my debt, so that by the time I finished university, I had no outstanding loans or debts. I was a free man, and even better, I was still alive.

After my dad died though, my thoughts of suicide were more concrete because, in my head, all fear had gone: as far as I was concerned, the very worst thing that could have happened to me had happened, and so I had nothing to lose.

One bad day rolled into another as I questioned God's very existence. If God had been there for me, he would have thrown me a lifeline by now; he would have gathered me up from my injured state and applied liniment to my wounds.

But he was nowhere to be seen.

I remember, in the hours before my dad died, walking out of his hospital room into the corridor for a breath of air. There was a family assembled, tears rolling down their cheeks, their heads close together, talking in low voices. I could tell they were a family on the verge of grief.

My immediate thought when I saw them was: *I pray that these people have you in their hearts, God.*

The reason I prayed like this was because I knew that, so long as they had God in their hearts, they had hope.

To me, hope equalled strength, optimism, and security.

In those dark days, when I was floundering in the dark for some sunlight, the absence of God was like the absence of hope. For as long as God lived in me, I had a purpose for living; if there was no God, what was the point of carrying on?

I was an empty shell.

These thoughts were occupying my mind one evening when I drove home from a gig along the motorway in the pitch dark. The road was uncharacteristically quiet – just me and the tarmac stretching far into the distance.

I wonder, I thought to myself, *what would happen if I drove into the crash barrier? What speed would I need to be doing for maximum impact?* My hands went limp on the steering wheel as if offering themselves submissively up to this crazy, fatal impulse.

There is a saying that 'the only reason we choose to stay alive is because we want to see what happens'.

Intense curiosity for what lay ahead in my future stopped me from veering sharply into the central reservation barrier, as if, with a tiny shake of my head, I woke up and was suddenly alive again and present, back in the hands of hope.

Was this God stepping in, lighting up the runway?

For several weeks afterwards, the question of God's existence permeated my mind: my faith was in the dock, up for scrutiny before a hard-nosed jury. There were days when I had hope and could breathe easy, and days when I was utterly lost and straining for air.

And then something happened that wrenched the isolated plots of solid ground out from beneath my feet.

One of the first friends I had made in Year 7 at St Edward's School was a girl called Daisy. Along with Joe, she had been my best friend. Together we formed a solid trio that carried us through school. We'd stayed in touch through the years and were still super close.

It had been a couple of months since I'd last seen Daisy, but we were in fairly constant communication. In fact, I'd messaged her the day before I got the call.

It was 19 December 2017. Joe often called me, so I didn't think anything of it.

'I've just spoken to Daisy's brother,' he said.

'Oh, yeah?' I replied. It wasn't much of a newsflash.

'Daisy's dead,' Joe said.

'What?' I grabbed my heart as it lurched in my chest. 'Why are you saying that?'

'I just can't believe it,' Joe said, his voice breaking.

Almost instantaneously memories of my life with Daisy started flooding back: the time when her, Joe, and me strolled all the way to school together after the bus didn't show up. That might not sound like a big deal, but if I were to tell you that the walk took three hours because it started in Ilford and ended five miles away in Romford, you would see what I mean. Knowing we had the no-show bus to use as our excuse, we walked very slowly, chatting and laughing all the way as if we had all the time in the world – which in those days we did.

Another memory: the first time Daisy met Emma in fact, when we were out having a Nando's in central London. Joe had a brainwave that we should all go away on holiday together. 'I'm up for it,' Daisy said, but then both she and Joe looked at me and Daisy said, 'You're gonna say you're up for it, Isaac, but something will come up last minute and you'll bottle.' She knew me well.

'I won't,' I said. 'I'm 100 per cent dedicated to the idea.'

'Prove it,' Daisy said.

I was so determined to show that I was committed that after the meal, I went to the cashpoint opposite the restaurant with Daisy and took out £300.

'Okay, that's my deposit.' I said.

Joe then did the same and Daisy left with £600 of guarantees in her pocket.

Holiday time approached and we were all set to go when, out of the blue, I was offered a gig to perform at Wembley – the Big W. I couldn't turn that down, could I?

'I knew you'd do that,' Daisy said.

'She passed away in her sleep,' Joe said into the phone, in answer to my silent question.

Whatever happened next has been erased from my brain. All I remember is that at some point in the minutes that passed, I fell to my knees and sobbed like I had never sobbed before.

Not Daisy. Oh God, not Daisy.

Daisy had been out at a work do the night before but didn't go overboard – nothing excessive as she was sensible. As she was diabetic she knew what she was doing, but for some reason, she died in her sleep due to complications caused by her diabetes.

The shock of Daisy's death came as an assault. In every second leading up to my dad's death, I'd had a lingering sense of hope: hope that God would come up trumps and carry him through. That was why I'd prayed.

With Daisy though, it was too late to act. By the time someone found her, she had gone – all hope extinguished before it ever had a chance to play its part. There was nothing I or anyone could have done.

It didn't help when two days after she died, on 21 December, I received her Christmas card signed Daisy, Dan, and Gatsby – Dan was her boyfriend of five years and Gatsby her dog (picture 15). She was always so good at sending out cards and thinking about people.

She was one of life's gentlest and sweetest people and left a huge hole in my heart.

I know what you're thinking, and yep, I do regret not taking that holiday, but I had no benefit of foresight and Wembley was a big deal.

With my dad's death I was as numb as a frostbitten toe; with Daisy, my sensory pathways were in overdrive, accepting every emotion that passed through and others that were not even directed my way. Having opened the gates, there was no chance I was shutting them down.

I was a mess. Emma told me later I was a mess in a good way, as this time I had the contents of the rubbish bin spread over the floor for all to see, not hidden away in corners out of sight.

Emma also told me that she knew I was handling Daisy's death better than my dad's because I was communicating with her. After my dad died, my feelings were so inverted and my armour so dense that it was impossible for anyone to come close. With Daisy though, I was up for being consoled. In fact, I needed it. There was no one patrolling my gates: all feelings had free movement to come and go as they pleased.

What's more, I found that I could be of help to others. Joe hadn't really experienced the death of anyone close and being just those few months ahead in the grieving process, I was able to support him.

Joe is very similar to me and I'm sure he benefitted

from having someone who understood what he was going through so close to hand, because – as I might have mentioned possibly once or twice through the course of this book – grief is a lonely, bewildering business.

'Feel what you feel, Joe. It's all a normal human response to trauma, bro.' It was as if my crash course in grief had happened for a reason.

It sounds heartless that I was even analysing my own journey through grief when my best friend's journey through life had ended so abruptly, but much of what I tell you now only became apparent to me months later, when a third tragedy forced me to gather my thoughts on the first two.

After Daisy died, my faith, which was already on shaky ground, was blown out of the water all over again. This time I didn't question God's existence, but I raged at his plan – openly raged.

It wasn't like the first time round when I'd blamed the world and the people in it, and nervously questioned God. This time, I let rip with my rage: 'Explain yourself!'

Reprimanding God so directly chilled me. God knew my soul inside out, nothing was hidden. I had never got angry with God before, but the tension between us was strong. I justified it by bringing to mind Psalm 22: 1–2, where David, feeling abandoned by God, cries: 'My God, my God, why have you forsaken me? Why are you so far from saving me, so far from my cries of anguish? My God, I cry out by day, but you do not answer, by night, but I find no rest.'

If David could lament God's plan, so could I. Where grief is something that we carry inside us, to suffer and endure, lamenting is our way of expressing that suffering. It is, in a sense, our song to God, beseeching him to reach out and offer us hope by answering our prayers.

Where are you God? I need you to be there right now.

All my life, I had sung in church, celebrated his wonders, his love, his greatness. I had found comfort in the words of Revelation 21: 4: 'He will wipe away every tear from their eyes, and death shall be no more, neither shall there be mourning, nor crying, nor pain anymore, for the former things have passed away.' But here, God was tearing lives apart, shattering hopes and dreams, dousing his faithful in unbearable sorrow.

At that point in time, I didn't feel like singing, looking for joy, or pleading to God. What I was looking for was permission to rage, permission to reprimand God for the harm he had done. Why did he have to cut short Daisy's life?

In March 2020, I made a really poignant podcast with the Archbishop of Canterbury, Justin Welby, for my *Loss Tapes* podcast series. In the interview he talked about his grief at losing his baby daughter in a car accident. I asked him if he was good at *lamenting*, as it is an important part of the loss and grief journey, especially when there is no explanation for the loss.

'I'm getting better at lamenting and protesting with God,' he told me and referred me to Psalm 44: 23–26, where the psalmist remonstrates against God's inaction:

Wake, Lord! Why do you sleep?
Rouse yourself! Do not reject us forever.
Why do you hide your face
    and forget our misery and oppression?
We are brought down to the dust;
    our bodies cling to the ground.
Rise up and help us;
    rescue us because of your unfailing love.

'Within modern Christianity,' he said, 'we are really bad at lament and protest; really bad at saying, this is terrible, this is wrong, this is awful; and we're really bad at saying, "God I am really mad about this. I am so angry about this. God, I think, you've let me down"'.

What that psalm teaches us is that it is okay to rage against God, even though it does not come easily to us. It is better to rage against him than to shut him out completely. In showing our true selves to God, he can reveal his true self to us. That is why lamenting and protesting in times of deep pain is as important as praising and celebrating in times of happiness. Learning to lament and protest is a journey towards better understanding God's love.

The archbishop also reminded me of something else, which I kind of knew instinctively already, but in the midst of my confusion following Daisy's death, I forgot to reflect on, and that is that bereavement is like a super-serious physical injury. He compared it to breaking your leg in nine places. If this happened, you wouldn't get up the next day and say, 'Right, I'm off for a walk'. You would start out cautiously on crutches, go to physio, wait for the injury to heal. The same applies when you lose someone close to you: you're in great pain and you need to give that pain time to heal.

Thanks to my grief counselling, I was better placed to manage my emotions after Daisy (picture 16). My counsellor enabled me to recognize the patterns I default to when I feel my life is out of control. By listening to what I had to say with his professional ear, he helped me locate the vocabulary for expressing how I felt.

I've always had it in me to want to help people. I'm a big brother, the eldest son. I found through the gift of writing that I can communicate and inspire, but I never expected that one day this desire would extend to supporting others in their grief. I suppose I never expected, or for that matter, thought about death coming into my life so early on. The way I saw it was that everything about my dad's death centred around me: *my* dad, *my* grief, *my* world torn apart. And apart from being some kind of a support to my mum, I was pretty much lost in my own bubble.

After Daisy died though, despite the rage I felt at God, I found my outlook took a far more selfless angle. I had lost a best friend, but so had Joe and countless other people: Daisy's brother had lost a sister; her parents had lost a child; and Dan and Gatsby had lost the love of their lives. With my newfound understanding of grief, I had a pretty clear picture of what everyone caught up in the shockwaves of Daisy's death would be experiencing: the disorientation; the yearning; the guilt; the torturous 'if onlys' and 'what ifs'; the constant search for meaning.

Although no two people grieve in the same way, most grief can be categorized using the same set of subheadings.

Most important for me was encouraging my friends to open up about what they were feeling, to talk openly, if not to friends and family, then to a professional. I know that I would have borne my initial grief so much better if I had done this sooner. Thanks to my own professional support, I had discovered a way of coping and I was aware that, second time around, this was my opportunity for getting things right.

I only found out several months later that apparently a few days after Daisy died, Emma had texted Nick saying: 'Please keep an eye on Isaac, as I am worried Daisy's death will tip him over the edge'.

When I reflect on this now, it shows how far unstuck

Emma and I had become if she was unable to share these concerns with me directly. This just goes to show that, even when I thought I was handling life more externally, I was still coming across as a closed book.

It was not long after Daisy's death that Emma suggested marriage counselling to help us find ways to resolve the conflict in our marriage. We bickered all the time and it was becoming our default, as neither of us knew how to break out of the cycle. I will tell you about this in more detail a little further on, but I will say here that what it revealed has been a good ride and made a massive difference to my life.

Firstly though, I'm gonna share with you the impact of the *online* world through the dark, difficult days of grief. Social media has played an enormous part in my professional life. I first launched my music on Myspace.com in 2006 when I was around seventeen, and it was the love, respect, and support of my friends and fans that got me out into the wider world enabling me to follow my dreams.

For this opportunity, I am truly grateful.

After my dad died, my reaction was to shut down completely, cut myself off from my marriage, best friends, and online 'family'. Communication of even the most superficial kind was painful for me. I wanted to protect myself, run away, and hide as my need for self-preservation was off the scale. At the same time, I knew that if I just flat-lined all my communication links with the outside world it would be unfair on the people who looked up to me.

As Guvna B, I am placed on a pedestal by many of my younger fans, who view me as a mentor and big brother. They love my music and respect what I stand for in terms of my positivity, faith, fight for justice, and success story. With my overwhelming grief, I knew that I was going to be out of sorts and out of action for a while, so I needed to explain why.

That's why the day after my dad died, on 18 July, I put out the following Instagram post and photograph (picture 17):

Rest in perfect peace Daddy. You're my G. Risked it all by moving over to London to set up shop and give the best possible life to your fam. The hardest worker I know and you did it without complaining. I'm gutted you didn't get to enjoy retirement. You always taught us about the importance of education and working hard so it's mad that you passed away a few days after you found out my lil bro secured the sickest Graduate's job. It's kinda like you knew your work was done cos your two boys are gonna do ok. 2 weeks ago everything was fine but life can change so quickly and I've got so many questions to ask God, but ultimately these are the moments where faith really has to get us through. P.S I promise to try my hardest to get into Formula 1 cos I know you'd be so gassed. And promise to look after Mummy too. Love you Pops.
(Instagram, 19 July 2017)

One single post to explain my radio silence. Much better that way than having to engage with everyone individually and repeat the same agonizing message over and over.

There is a lot written on the positives and negatives of sharing grief online. In Western culture, grief is often kept under wraps, to be done within the four walls of home, a sort of 'move on, nothing to see here' mentality. In Ghanaian culture, as I mentioned before, death is colourful, passionate, and emotional, yet celebratory.

Sharing my dad's death with the wider community felt like I was fusing my two cultures together: managing what

I was putting out there about my dad, but at the same time, celebrating his life by sharing his photo and my feelings about what he meant to me.

The response of love, support, wishes was overwhelming. The only people who minded a bit were a couple of 'life' friends, who complained that they'd found out more about what I was going through online than from the twenty per cent I put out when we met up for a drink. Sorry about that, but as my friends, you know better than most what I'm like.

A couple of months later, I did a follow-up post:

Yoooo, huge thanks for all the prayers and kind messages over the last few weeks. Really appreciate it. It's easy to have faith when things are going well, but in tough times you find out what you truly believe. When it's been tough to pray and have faith I've pulled through because I'm still choosing to trust that God's got a plan regardless. That doesn't mean we won't have ups and downs, just means that no matter what life chucks our way, we're never alone and all things will work out for good. Apologies for any shows that had to be cancelled. Looking forward to getting back on the road and making pops proud.
(Instagram, 8 September 2017)

By sharing my grief journey in this way, I liked to think that I was putting the message out that it's okay to admit to vulnerability and sadness, and to question God. We all need to do it from time to time and to feel safe and supported enough to do so. I also knew that my grief was not going anywhere any time soon. In fact, something I learnt from my counselling is that grief never goes away; I just have to learn to live with it. It was important to me that people understood that my dad's death had triggered a shift in my outlook and mindset that was here to stay.

When Daisy died, I had to share it. I wanted people to know that a sparkling light had been extinguished from my world (picture 18).

'In a world where you can be anything, be kind.' – @msdaisymorgan. My family since year 7. Rest In Peace you beautiful soul
(Instagram, 19 December 2017)

The response to the above post was unprecedented. With my dad, the messages of support had been aimed at me, but when Daisy died, it was as if everyone, everywhere, felt free to open up and share their own stories of grief and loss. Daisy's death triggered a huge feeling of love, solidarity, and openness; it was as if she was radiating the joy that had carried her through her life from high in the heavens above. All of the messages thanked me for being so honest and letting people know that they were not alone.

I found that by sharing my grief with my fans, or 'extended family', as I prefer to think of them, I was so much more effective at revealing what I really felt than I was in real life. Prior to my dad's passing, I had always feared opening up and telling it like it was, as offering my soul in raw form was out of keeping with the image people had of me.

Until then, I was known as an inspiration, for my uplifting, positive outlook on life. As the new Isaac, I was a *deeper* version of my former self. It was as if I had only tapped into forty per cent of who I was, and I was only now beginning to peel back the layers.

Sharing what I was going through acted like a form of counselling and comfort. It was as if I was saying, 'Okay, here I am in my hour of need. Take me or leave me. Either way, I'm going to tell it like it is.' I believe that being honest like this went a long way towards helping me through, and not only me, but other people too.

So yeah, 2017 was my worst year ever, which was why, on 30 December 2017, I posted this cheery little New Year's message:

> I grew up hearing so many sick new year statements like 'Next year is gonna be your year! All your dreams are gonna come true etc.' Then I'd pray to God and ask Him to make all my wildest dreams come true and all that good stuff. But 2017 has been a weird one for me. It's been a year of extreme highs and extreme lows and to be honest the lows have taught me more than the highs.
> Sometimes we get gassed by the glamorous stuff. For example, success in your career, more money, more plantain & chicken or whatever other things you want to see happen in your life. But this year has been my most successful because it's been my worst, but i made it through.
> I don't know much but my bit of advice: if 2018 doesn't work out how you planned, just try to make it through and don't give up. Sometimes it's not where the journey takes you, it's who the journey makes you.
> This is the most depressing New Year's message ever init? I'm working on having a more positive outlook on life. I know God's got our backs through the good and the bad. Have a good year and try and be grateful for all of it because no one owes us anything. Take the rough with the smooth, keep ya

head up and give thanks EVERYDAY!
(Instagram, 30 December 2017)

This was the new Guvna B talking, bearing my soul and pulling no punches.

9. ANOTHER HIT

When Emma suggested we go for marriage counselling, I was surprised.

'Why?'

'I think we could do with some support.'

I had never doubted the strength of my marriage. I knew that whatever life threw our way, I would always have Emma's back and she would have mine. Emma didn't see it quite as so clear-cut: she cited statistics on the impact of grief on divorce and the benefit of counselling on marriages. I was quite slow to pick up on her hints.

'If you want to go …' I said.

'It's not a case of *wanting* to go. It's something we *need* to do.'

'Okay.'

Passivity is my middle name – you know that by now – which is why I agreed to it. In my work I am all get up and go, keep moving, keep improving. In my married life, I am (ashamedly) more of the mindset, 'Anything for a peaceful life.' If it had been left up to me, I most probably would have carried on with the quarrelling and squabbling, as it would never have crossed my mind to come up with an alternative.

It had been a couple of months since I had ended my

sessions with the bereavement counsellor because we had come to the end of the road. Helpful as they were, there was only so much I had to say about losing my dad. I wasn't convinced there was much I could say about my marriage either, but Emma and I were introduced to a marriage counsellor offering solution-based counselling, which meant a bit less talking and more practical action points.

Many couples never view marriage counselling as an option and go straight to the divorce courts; others view it as something to turn to when times are desperate – a last-ditch attempt at rescuing a marriage. I'm not quite sure either was the case for Emma and me. Our marriage had never reached desperate stakes; we were pretty solid in our love for, and commitment to, one another. We just didn't have any of the coping skills in place for resolving the conflicts that arose between us.

Even before turning up and sitting on the counsellor's couch, I knew that the majority of the problems in our marriage were based around my lack of communication. Successful marriages are built on communication. You can always tell when a marriage is on the rocks when someone says, 'We just don't communicate any more'. I guess that was our problem, except I had never communicated very much to start with.

Anyway, I was right. Within a few minutes of turning up, the counsellor had recognized me as a 'hedgehog'; someone who, when faced with conflict, instinctively curled into a prickly ball of self-defence and hid their head. Emma, on the other hand, was identified as a 'rhino', approaching conflict head on, horns out, and primed to fight.

I reckon if I did a count of the amount of times that I have mentioned communication in this book, you'd think I was the world's best communicator. LOL! In actual fact, it was not until I started going to marriage counselling that I properly understood what communication is. No, really! I had always thought that communication was about imparting how I felt, sharing my thoughts, talking to people, and opening up. That is why the word has always bothered me because none of the above came naturally.

In reality, nearly half of all communication is made up of *listening*. That's why we've got two ears and only one mouth, innit! (Mum taught me that one.) Failure to listen properly means misinterpreting what is being said.

I have always considered myself quite a good listener. I prefer hearing people talk about themselves to me doing all the talking, but when it came to me and Emma in conflict mode, my natural defence was to shut down and stop listening. In actual fact, it was something the counsellor identified as a mutual problem for both of us. I didn't listen to Emma's words and Emma didn't listen to my silence.

Hearing the counsellor identify the issues between me and Emma was intense. I suppose they had always been present, but it was not until my dad died that my silence had reached deafening decibels, triggering the need to act.

You think you know someone back to front and inside out, but often you can only see life from the constraints of your own perspective. Learning all this stuff about how Emma and I tick showed me how complex human beings are, and how conditioned we are by our upbringing.

Before counselling, for example, I never knew that birth order can have an impact on marriage. I am the eldest child. I spent the first six years of my life as an only child until my brother was born, so I'm quite self-sufficient and used to being by myself. Emma has two older sisters – she's the baby – so when she was born, she was immersed straight into family life and had to carve her path, so she's used to thinking and acting with a pack mentality.

Then, there is the matter of culture. As I said before, Emma was brought up eating her meals around a dining table, whereas I was brought up eating my meals alone; I was brought up to listen and accept, Emma was brought up to talk and question.

It's true – this stuff makes a difference. As soon as it was pointed out, it all made sense.

Most revealing of all though were the love languages. (If this is all getting too intimate for you, you have my full permission to skip a few pages. Otherwise, stick with me, as this might apply to you too.)

There are five love languages and our counsellor asked us which two we looked for in love:

1. Quality time;
2. Acts of service;
3. Buying of gifts;
4. Words of affirmation;
5. Physical touch.

I picked: acts of service and physical touch.

Emma chose: quality time and words of affirmation.

That meant that we both had different views on what was important in our love for one another. Emma valued me having a day off over whether I tidied the house from top to bottom, whereas I valued a clean house over having a day off.

Until we knew about love languages, we were always bickering about the same stuff without any idea of how to get around it. Now we both know better what is important to the other and so we can be aware of it. I'm not saying we get it right 100 per cent of the time. There's a lot of room for error, but before we default to getting mad at each other, I

can now take a step back and go, 'Oh yeah, you know what ...
Emma's upset because she doesn't like it when I spend my
precious time off looking at my phone', or Emma might think,
'I'd rather we were out spending quality time together, but
Isaac would prefer his favourite meal so let me make that.'

Since counselling we know each other better and what
works for us. In arguments, Emma always used to expect
me to react immediately to whatever she had to say, and
when I didn't, she would get annoyed and accuse me of not
caring. I can't react instantly, as it sends my hedgehog into
overdrive. So now, she allows me time out to reflect on the
points she is putting across, which means I can provide a
much more measured, thoughtful response.

We still go for counselling every now and again, mainly
when we have a barney. Ha! Just the other week, we were
stuck in a row of oversized proportions – mad, bad, and
ugly. When we got to counselling, the counsellor asked,
'So, what's going on here?' Me and Emma looked at each
other and we just burst out laughing, as neither of us could
remember what we were arguing about.

So, you see, I'm something of a convert. From growing
up in a family where no one opened up to internal strife,
unless it was to God, I have come full circle and now find
relief and comfort in having a professional do what they do
so well. I'm thankful to Emma for encouraging this.

It took me a while to own up to my mum that I was
seeking help, as I was certain that not only would she
disapprove, but she would also worry about how bad it had
got for me to go to such desperate measures. When I did
'fess up it was because I wanted to encourage her to speak
to someone for herself, as I believed it would help her if she
found some release. I now believe that no one should go
through life bearing worry, anxiety or grief alone.

I'm pretty sure not too many people in my family have gone to counselling, which is a shame as it would provide an opportunity to change the narrative for all of us going forward into the next generation, which would be a good thing. It has definitely done that for me 100 per cent.

In my New Year 2017/18 post I stated that I was going to try and get myself a more positive outlook for 2018, and I did. It turned out to be a much better year than I could have predicted, mainly because of the impact *Hands are Made for Working* had on so many lives. The album tapped into broken hearts and lost, confused souls crying out for someone or something to relate to. One of the most touching letters I got was from a fan who wrote to tell me that 'King of my Heart', the twelfth track on the album, had stopped her from self-harming. She had struggled with this for eight years due to feelings of worthlessness, but the song enabled her to find her inner soul and unravel a sense of self-worth.

Hearing that meant the world to me: even if I had zero in the bank and no-shows at my gigs, I would still consider that album worth every ounce of its weight in gold for that reaction alone.

King of my Heart

Even when I don't understand your ways
I know there's no one taking your place
You control the breaths that we take
And that's hard
Cos 2017 left scars
Dad passed, and then Daisy. Both had my heart
Can't leave those thoughts in the past

Still put my trust in you
Hope heaven's got a place for the crew
I know you're gonna come through
Cos there ain't nothing you can't do
So I call you king of my heart
I'd give you my last breath

Finding light at the end of a long, dark tunnel meant that when I was hit by a third tragedy in my life, I was strong enough to bear it.

This time, like the last two times, I got a phone call out of the blue, from Franklyn's flatmate Jay. Franklyn had been one of my four housemates at university and we had lived together for two years. He had a liver disease, which meant he was not in the finest of health, but he should not have died. He was just over thirty and in the prime of his life.

Franklyn was the most unassuming, gracious man. We were both on the same business course at university, and both had our foot equally off the pedal when it came to completing our coursework on time. I know that because the night before we were due to hand in the coursework that we'd had months to prepare, the only people working like crazy all night long were me and him.

'Do you want to come around and see him before they take him away?' Jay asked me.

Course I did: I wanted to pay my respects. I got straight into my car and tapped his postcode into my satnav. It came up telling me that I would be there in twenty minutes.

I called Jay. 'I'll be there in twenty.'

Saying that was when it struck me how close I lived to Franklyn, but how little I had seen him in the years since we'd left university. Twenty minutes: it takes longer than that to go to the supermarket; longer than that to cook a breakfast fry-up. We always said we would meet more, but I never got around to making it happen, and it had to come from me as I was the one that packed my life to the seams.

When me and Emma got married, we wanted to have a small wedding, with just close family and friends, followed by a big wedding party in the evening. We had to make the tough decision on who to invite for the whole event and who would come later. The first person who popped into my mind as someone who would not mind missing the ceremony was Franklyn. He was a big-hearted, amiable character and I knew that he would understand. When I called him to tell him what we were planning, he accepted it straight off, saying he understood, and no, he wasn't offended, and yes, he knew that I valued him as one of my closest friends. I thought I'd got my message across but then, just to do a bit of stirring, Franklyn wrote a post on our university flatmate WhatsApp group, dissing me: 'Calls me his friend, but doesn't even want me at his wedding ceremony.'

He was joking, I knew that, but that didn't stop the rest of the group all wading in and mocking me about it for years after.

I drove fast, wondering why I'd never put the same sense of urgency into visiting my friend when he was alive.

Why was my life so busy that I had never put twenty minutes aside before to drive over to see someone I regarded highly?

What did it say about me and where my values lay?

It was with my mate Franklyn in mind that I wrote 'Kumbaya' in his memory.

Kumbaya
Seven in the evening,
Sitting in a yard with my head up to the ceiling,

I need healing.
Daydreaming,
Can't shake the feeling I should have been there for
    my friends when they needed.
Can't believe it, that's my brother Fisko.
W-we used to two-step at the disco.
Na I mean the rave, we weren't listening to Sisqo,
    cause it was Funky House. Got low like the limbo.
Saw him at the Kevin Hart Show. We got about.
Said he's been in hospital, but they let him out.
I said, 'Cuz, that's mad. I gotta come to your house.'
He was down, he said, 'Cool' no doubt, but
It's too late.
Same old story:
Never made time, found su'tt'in' more important.
A twenty minute drive and I couldn't even manage, but
    the night of when he died, I was there in a panic.
I should've made time when he had it,
But now it's too late and it's tragic.
Feels like a habit.
Said I should've made time when he had it,
But now it's too late, and it's tragic
Feels like a habit.

Kumbayah
Singing 'Kumbayah-yah-yeah'
Yesterday's history.
Tomorrow is a mystery.
Today we're singing
Kumbayah.
Singing 'Kumbayah-yah-yeah'
Yesterday's history.
Today, that's a gift, G.

Franklyn died almost twelve months to the day after Daisy – the third catastrophic loss from my life in less than eighteen months. Was this going to be my experience from now on? Was death going to be a fact of life now that I was leaving my youth behind? I couldn't believe that. I was just unlucky. Maybe God was punishing me for a reason. That felt more probable. Was this God's way of getting me to value the people dear to me in my life? I had let three special people slip through the net. The message I was receiving loud and clear was to make time for the people that matter, because we never knew how long we'd got together living side by side on this earth.

After Dad and Daisy died, I was in shock mode because it had never crossed my mind that the people I loved would not live forever. I was naively of the belief that everyone important to me would live a long, rich life and die in old age, happily ever after. I was in Fairytale Land.

By the time it got to Franklyn though, all that naivety had been swept away with a wire-haired brush. I was a Death Veteran now. I knew how his death was going to hit me, and I was ready. That doesn't mean to say it didn't have an impact. In fact, Franklyn's death was as much a lesson as the previous two, because it not only showed me how important it was to appreciate everyone I loved, but it also removed the rose-tinted spectacles I had worn all my life and replaced them with a dustier, grittier pair that obscured my unfiltered optimism. Once bitten, twice shy … three times uneasy (picture 19).

Today we lay to rest my brother Fisko. Not many people more clean hearted than him. Always the first to show love, make peace, stay positive. Gonna miss you dissing my hairline and my dress sense. Probably

looking down today thinking 'Guv, how you gonna come to my funeral with that hairline & those shoes'. Love you forever brother.
(Instagram, 4 December 2018)

I was reluctant to put my trust into lasting relationships as I was scared of being hurt. Before, if I'd heard about someone being admitted to hospital, my default would have been to think positively: 'They will be pull through. No doubt'. After Franklyn, my default was to assume the worst. In some ways that was good, because it got me praying 'not another one Lord, please', but at the same time, the fragility of life left me unsettled.

Unlike with Dad and Daisy, Franklyn's death didn't find me questioning God. I never doubted him. In fact, Franklyn dying made me feel closer to God than I had in a very long time. I can't fully explain why. It was as if through this third tragic death, God was giving me a bigger perspective on life.

Let me put it like this: when my dad died, my grief revolved around *me*; all eyes turned inwards. When Daisy died, I was able to disentangle myself from myself and offer support to other people.

But when Franklyn died, I grew up. I got to see life with all its cuts and bruises and that enabled me to be strong. I realized that to be the best we can be, and to enjoy the wonders of life, we have to endure the flipside of pain and loss.

In John 10: 10, Jesus promised to give us life to the full: 'I come that they might have life and that they might have it more abundantly.' I used to interpret this as him giving us an amazing life, full of highs. And yes, God does want us to have an amazing life. But now, after experiencing grief for

Dad, Daisy, and Franklyn, I view the verse differently. I think that life to the full can sometimes mean 'the fullness of joy', but it can equally mean the fullness of sadness. Don't get me wrong, I would give anything to have any one of those three people back, but in looking for a reason or a purpose in God's plan, that is what I have come up with.

Someone asked me recently whether I feel I am a better person for having come through the grief.

My answer was: No, probably not. A better person would have put aside time to spend with these three vital people when they were alive.

But am I a different person for it? Yes, I am – 1,000 per cent.

Three deaths in eighteen months focus the mind. When living on the estate, I had hovered on the outskirts of death all my life, and it sometimes came close enough for me to track its scent, but until it hit me so personally I had never realized quite how painful it is and how it changes a person. People often talk about 'coming out of the fog of grief', 'waking up and feeling better', or 'recovering from grief'. In my experience, none of these events have happened. For me, it is much more as if I have *accepted* the grief as a part of me, and learnt to live with it.

I told you earlier how my dad's death triggered a shift in my mindset and outlook, but it also triggered a shift in my life, as it seemed that everything that I turned my hand to suddenly started working in my favour.

I was learning to listen to my true self and trust my instincts. It was a long time since I'd had the guts to do this. Most probably the last time I'd trusted my instincts was when I'd agreed to meet Emma in 2013 after seeing her photo. I'd had a good feeling about her, went with it, and a lifelong love affair was born. In the rest of my life, though, my insecurity and overthinking made me too cautious. Too many 'what ifs' and 'buts', and not enough, 'I will' and 'I can'.

With my dad's, Daisy's, and Franklyn's passing it was time to throw caution to the wind. What is more, I could sense God by my side rooting for me, steering and guiding me in my action plan. The words of Romans 8: 28 suddenly had more meaning: 'And we know that all things work together for good to them that love God, to them who are the called according to his purpose.'

What I came to learn, not always easily, is that there is never a smooth path with faith, and I don't think that anything that comes without some sort of trial is worth having. What I am now sure of is that God would never give me or anyone else anything that they couldn't take on board and handle. We've just got to keep going and wait for God to open the doors; keep our faith through the hard times, at one in the knowledge that God is working for us.

When I released *Hands are Made for Working*, a whole new channel of communication was opened up between me and all those people who found comfort and understanding through my music. Without living through the grief, those channels would have remained untapped.

A lot of people who don't like rap or grime turn to my music because it breaks through the stereotypical view many people have of rap and grime, by offering clean content with an honest message.

One of the most amazing pieces of feedback I ever received was when someone wrote to me saying they had listened to my album and it 'spoke to them when they had no words'.

It is hard for me to imagine now how my life would have played out if I had not been blessed with the opportunity to connect with people on this deeper level.

There is so much positivity that comes out of holding up a mirror to how we truly feel. I compare being able to speak the rawest truth without fear of judgement to flying without wings.

10. LET IT OUT

On 15 June 2017, exactly one month before my dad died, my first book, *Unpopular Culture*, was published by SPCK Publishing. I was inspired to write the book after seeing a billboard at my train station that read, 'Be Number One.' It got me wondering: *Is that what life is all about? Being number one, making loads of money, getting the best job? What if there is another way to live; one that involves us living life for more than just ourselves, even if it means going against the grain and carving out our own route?* The book is a call to young people to look at the world and the people around them more positively, to find a faith, and live up to their God-given potential, even if it means risking unpopularity in the process.

The fact that *Unpopular Culture* became an Amazon bestseller indicates that it was a book young people felt they needed – and not only the young. Meet ninety-one-year-old Sheila (picture 20):

Sheila, 91 years old. Saw me on TV and heard my story then bought my book. After reading it, she wrote 'pass it on' on the inside cover and gave it to her grandchild. One of her favourite songs is Nothing

But the Blood and she's prayed for me ever since she found out about me. This world has some incredible people in it. More people are rooting for you than you think and more people are praying for you than you think. Keep going. Cheers Sheila
(Instagram, 27 July 2018)

When I wrote *Unpopular Culture*, I had no idea that my dad's heart was pumping its final beats in time to the rhythm of life. I thought I had the world sorted, that I had reached adulthood unscathed, and that, even though I didn't have all the answers, I was at least able to locate the tools for accessing them.

On 18 July 2017, the day my life turned upside down, it hit me that, in fact, I hardly knew myself at all. Everything I had talked about in *Unpopular Culture*, in relation to taking control, trusting in God, and becoming emotionally aware, dissolved before my eyes.

It was as if someone had grabbed hold of the steering wheel and driven me into a ditch. I sat dazed and confused before eventually picking myself up, brushing off the leaves and twigs, and figuring out who and where I was.

What I discovered as a result of my dad dying was that I struggled with rage and loneliness, because I didn't understand the importance of talking about my feelings. I thought that if I showed people, even those closest to me, how I was properly hurting, they would see me as weak and vulnerable, and that went against the lifelong conditioning I'd had drummed into me – that men are strong; men take it on the chin; and most importantly of all ... men don't cry.

It is actually quite surprising that I was so out of touch with my true self considering I had been using my lyrics and music as a form of personal expression for so many years.

In 2011, I released my mixtape, *Scrapbook*, which was like my personal diary in rap form and documented the trials and tribulations of being a young person of faith in a broken world. In this, I believed I was opening up – not all the way, but just enough of the way to reveal a little of who I was.

I received so many messages after the album dropped, from people telling me that they related 100 per cent to everything I had to say, that I discovered my music could act as some sort of lifeline for young people in need of direction.

Skin Deep

So many faces we see every day of our lives,
On the road, in cars, on trains, to the left, to the right.
Who knows what lies inside as I write this rhyme.
Somebody in the world's dying right now,
And somebody's smiling right now,
And somebody's listening, so I can't put the mic down.
We only see we're skin deep, and nobody knows
     what's in deep.

Pain can hide behind a smile, a laugh can hide away
     the strain,
But it will fade after a while, you'll have to deal with
     it again.
And life's a big rainbow, the sunshine works with
     the rain.

It's skin deep, nobody knows what's in deep.
They only see me from the outside, and they don't
     know the struggle I try to hide.

It's skin deep, that's all they see from where their feet
    are,
But in my heart is so much deeper, I know that I've
    got much more to show …

Sometimes, it's safer to hold it all in,
Where the only person who can judge you is yourself.
Have you ever walked into a place full of so many
    people and still felt lonely?

In my next few albums, I improved on this by baring more of my inner thoughts and addressing many of the issues affecting young people growing up today. However, the words, though they seemed heartfelt at the time, did not come direct from the bottom of my heart, but instead, from a little corner I had fenced off after identifying it as a part of me that was safe to reveal.

What's weird is that I didn't know I was holding back at the time. I thought that I was operating at 100 per cent and giving it all I had. It was only with my dad's death, and when writing the lyrics for *Hands are Made for Working*, that I realized that what I had been putting out before was at most only seventy per cent honest and true.

It was only because I lost all sense of fear of how I might be judged that I dared to go so far to reveal my authentic self.

That it should take something as extreme as the death of a loved one for me to 'man up' enough to expose my full emotional palette shows how debilitated I was by my *conditioning*, which the *Collins Dictionary* defines as 'the learning process by which the behaviour of an organism becomes dependent on an event occurring in its environment'.

I am in the highly fortunate position of being granted

permission to bare my soul for a living, and exceptionally privileged in being paid to do so. Yet it took seven years from the release of *Scrapbook* to the release of *Hands are Made for Working* for me to find the courage to 'go real'.

If that is how hard it was for me, what can be expected of young men growing up in a culture where masculine toxicity is their reality? Men who lack any kind of outlet to express themselves, where even the simplest flicker of emotion lays them open at best to ridicule, and at worst – and possibly more likely – to assault or even death.

In 2013, I was booked to play one of the biggest gigs I'd ever performed at, to a couple of thousand people in one of the after-hours music venues at a festival called @soulsurvivoruk. I remember being super nervous, but that night was the start of a special bond between me and the 'Soul Survivor' crew and was more than just a 'gig'. I went back pretty much every year until it ended.

> Yesterday marked the last SS [Soul Survivor] ever. I've got so many sick memories. Doing my first (and last) stage dive is one of them. I ended up on the floor and chipped two teeth. Suppose it's my fault for choosing to dive into a group of 15 year old girls… Didn't really think that through did i? Anyway I've probably seen over 100,000 young people at SS over the years but the best memories come from the one-on-one stories. Meeting young people who have battled on through anxiety, depression, self-harm, grief, youth violence, addictions and even still never gave up. They chose to have faith for better days. Thank you. To everyone that I've ever met at SS over the years, you've made way more of an impact on me than you

think. Thanks for the love and keep fighting my G's
(Instagram, 28 August 2019)

When I was growing up there was violence on the estate where I lived, but most of the time it didn't lead to fatalities. People carried knives and guns, but more for protection, or as symbols of status, than to use for brutal means. I had just turned eleven, when ten-year-old Damilola Taylor was stabbed to death on the North Peckham Estate in 2000, which was the biggest news story of the month. I reckon if you ask most people of my age and older what they were doing the day they heard about Damilola Taylor, a large proportion of them will be able to remember. It was so unusual that it scarred the nation.

In 2019, twenty-three teenagers were fatally stabbed in London alone, and I doubt most people would be able to remember one of the victims' names. Youth homicide is at a record high, with the majority of victims and perpetrators registered as young men aged sixteen to twenty-four.

When a young person is fatally stabbed or shot, it instantly becomes a mental-health issue for their friends, family, and the wider community as the grief manifests as depression, anger, and anxiety.

This needs to be addressed, as otherwise, if you brush a problem under the carpet, you get a bumpy carpet.

Between 2014 and 2018, there was a 300 per cent increase in demand for youth mental-health services at St George's Hospital, Tooting, with four out of ten of the young people who applied for a place being turned away. According to the NSPCC, the soar in demand ties in with the increase, at around this time, in the frequency of youth violent crime.

For all the people seeking help for their mental health,

there are just as many refusing to go down that route: people like me, whose default in times of adversity is to withdraw, lose themselves inside their head, and shut themselves away; the same people who, on the surface, look like they are holding it all together:

'How are you?'

'I'm *fine*.'

The same people who feel numb and emotionless, who struggle even to let out a tear, too worried about their control unravelling to loosen the knot.

It's a lesser-known fact that young people process death more slowly than adults, which means they might look fine straight after the event and so everyone rests easy, but they are then hit with the pain and grief later on, when the event has passed and the empathy gone.

It is the young people whose grief goes unchecked that we need to worry about, because they are the ones most likely to become angry, irrational, and impulsive, or silent, withdrawn, and excluded from school – the ones we mark out as *dangerous* or *criminal*, when in reality, they are the ones feeling the most lost and alone, dejected and worthless.

Essentially, they are the ones crying out for our help.

When people die, there is a lot of talk about the death and the life, but not much talk about the grief that comes as a consequence. Until grief hits, you don't really consider that it might affect you. It's a bit like going to a restaurant, eating the meal, and leaving without giving a thought to the person cleaning up. When young people feel angry, depressed, or anxious after a death, they don't understand that as *grief*, unless people explain it to them. They just feel the emotions that come as a consequence of grief and, depending on their perspective, either engage with them or bury them deep.

When I was fifteen, one of my friends from the estate was fatally stabbed. I remember feeling completely shocked when it happened, as that was as close as I had ever come to that level of violence. The next day, though, life kind of went on as normal: it might have felt strange just continuing, but I didn't have much previous experience to know if this was 'normal' or not. Me and my friends spoke about the stabbing from the sensationalist angle – how it happened, where it happened, the blood, the perpetrators – but there wasn't any shared sense of mourning. The attitude was almost like, 'Lost another one, life goes on.'

I was hurting, I know that, and for a while I was scared, suddenly fearful of my own mortality. My parents knew about the stabbing, but they never sat me down to talk to me about how it was affecting me. No one ever said, 'You're going to be affected by this death, Isaac. You will find that life looks different for a while.'

After a week or so, the world seemingly returned to normal – at least, for his friends and the wider community it did. I doubt the same could be said for his parents. No family ever gets over the death of a loved one, but everyone else just continued on as normal, burying the wounds and filling the space that our friend had occupied. I wrote about the tragedy of young deaths in 'Cushty' (see lyrics below).

Knowing what I know now about loss, it seems strange that not once through this whole tragic event was the word 'grief' ever mentioned.

Cushty

Free school dinners
Pops didn't have no Beamer.
Cuz didn't have no figure

That's why he roll with the olders, strap to your dome,
    see dome get lick off
But nobody's a winner
Mum broke down in Tesco, she won't ever see her
    son get bigger
So, can't jus' flip that flow, nah, I'm gonna flip that mode.
Big boy strap and the kickback loads
Ten years old when he hit that road
There's gotta be another way, cah I need man home
    for Mother's Day.
So like, she's one hug away, gotta turn our back on
    our stubborn ways

It's kickin' off in East, told young G, 'Never back that beef'.
Why? I don't wanna see man bleed.
So, out 'ere turnin' cheeks.
An' I know it ain't easy, streets be greazy and that's
    each, year, weeks, yeah.
Days in the ends be bleak, yeah.
Brothers in the back of the Jeep, yeah.
Tinted whip, can't see clear,
Out on the strip, better beware
Look at that boy with a deep stare.
Run man down's what they teach here.
Hard on the roads an' it's peak, prayer
Youths in the ends, got talent an' skill, gotta plan it an'
    build an' achieve their's
Too many lives been lost on the roads, and I don't
    wanna see a man reap tears.
Tell a man, 'It's all love' when I pass through time, time
    we evolve see peace here
North, west, south to the east, know that.
Everything Cushty

As I've said before, I was not a particularly likeable person to be around when my dad died, but I had a strong network of friends and family that carried me through and gave me all the support I needed. It is thanks to them sticking with me and putting up with me that I was able to move forward. Having people to talk to is just as vital for young people, except that this requires, first off, having an adult to talk to, and second, being willing to talk. Part of the process of growing up involves pushing away those people who care about you the most, in order to seek some independence. That's why teenagers experiencing trauma often fall through the net when it comes to opening up about how they feel.

Believe it or not, I have very few clear memories from the year or so after my dad died, just snippets here and there, but most of my coherent thoughts are pretty piecemeal.

I understand now that this is a version of self-preservation. As so much of what I was experiencing was painful, it was like my brain was offering me only bitesize memories to chew on and mull over, while preventing the whole onrush from being processed at once. It was only when I made the space to reflect and understand, alongside receiving love and counselling, that the remainder of my memories could be drip-fed to me in small doses, with time between each one to allow for processing. Despite all the support, much of that period still remains a blur. That is why it is important to work through your grief, otherwise the memories and emotions get buried and the grief is never properly resolved.

The fact that I can talk about my dad's death and the death of my friends now is because I realized through the process of my grief that if I didn't open up, I would never fully understand how I was feeling, which would subsequently mean I was limiting myself from ever reaching my full potential.

I had to learn, and I had to grow. That was the only way forward.

The reason my grief got complicated and I became depressed was because I was too independent, too stubborn, or too naive perhaps, to work through the steps to resolve it. Refusing to talk about the loss of a loved one is a sure sign of unresolved grief, as is avoiding making new relationships because of the fear of being hurt and 'moving on' without looking back. Whichever way you look (and half the time people don't look at all) unresolved grief can lead to unexplained mental-health problems later on.

I suppose it is also worth mentioning that the way we learn about death, mourning, and grief is changing. When I was growing up, social media was not like it is now. To put it in perspective for you, I was fifteen years old when Facebook was launched, twenty-one years old with Instagram, and twenty-two years old with Snapchat. Believe it or not, these platforms haven't been around forever. That meant that previously, news travelled very slowly. The only time you heard anyone say 'viral' was in connection with a health condition, and 'word on the street' was 'word of mouth'. That meant that to find out what was going on you had to *speak* to people directly, or catch it on the news.

In 2016 – we're back in the modern day now – I was at the massive Newday Festival at Norfolk Showground, in Norwich. There were loads of young people there, all under-18s, including a group from a South London youth club. On the night I was performing, a well-known friend of the crowd from South London was fatally stabbed. That alone was tragic, but what made the whole shock and sadness ten times worse was that the stabbing was filmed, and the video of the victim lying dead was then circulated online. The video spread like wildfire and had gone viral before some of the victim's family had even found out.

I'm not going to lie – it was horrible.

The festival campsite was filled with hundreds of twelve to sixteen-year-olds in varying states of distress as the video came to light. Some were screaming, others sobbing, whereas others were holding it in, anaesthetized by shock. It was mayhem. What do you do in that situation? The event staff had to transform instantly from bouncers and gatekeepers into counsellors to deal with the mass fallout of anguish.

No one was equipped to deal with that level of horror. Thanks to Snapchat, it was out of control. How can you tell young people that the world is looking out for them and is on their side, when they are witnessing images of this nature?

However, this all happened before my dad died, before I had any idea of how people are affected in the aftermath of death.

My shock and horror was for the then and there. How were they going to calm down? How were they going to get through the night? How were they going to erase that gruesome image from their minds? I had no idea then that this was only the start of a long, painful journey through healing. I am prepared to wager that the majority of those kids are still suffering the impact of that experience today, with pretty major effects on their mental health, but I'm not certain many of them will connect the way they feel now with the grief triggered by the shock and sadness at finding out about the loss of their friend.

Society isn't great at coming to the rescue in times of sorrow, as grief is too shapeless and personal to pinpoint and there are no quick-fix solutions – and society likes a quick fix.

Also, we have all become rather desensitized when it comes to violent deaths. Sometimes fatal stabbings don't even get a mention on the news. If society doesn't clock tragic deaths and manage the outcome, how can we expect young people to deal with the pain?

Those of you who have been with me on the Guvna B journey from the start will know how passionate I am about young people finding their faith and having someone to believe in them. I see my role, both through my words and music, as being like an older brother to young people as they forge their path into adulthood. Where parents are absent or out of touch, older siblings, being just that bit further ahead in their own journey, have the benefit of both foresight and hindsight: they know the world their younger siblings inhabit, and chances are they have been through the same experiences and discovered what works for them.

A lot of my work involves going into schools and youth clubs, talking to young people about my life and experiences – that is, being that big brother with a positive narrative. I imagine that the stories I tell are not that different from the stories they hear from their teachers every day of the school year. But to many of the young people I address, I look like their potential future – I'm not a lawyer or doctor dressed in a suit or a white coat; I'm a rapper. I make music that deals with their world, and I wear trainers. LOL!

There are many misconceptions relating to black people in our society and I feel I have a role to play in setting the record straight, acting as a role model, listening to what people have to say, and showing them that it is okay to express how they feel.

Youth workers, and people like me who work a lot with young people, need to let it be known that the door for talking to us is always open. Sometimes in putting out the same message, we run the risk of slipping into autopilot and forgetting the important role we have to play in young people's lives. It is very important that we never lose sight of the difference we can make simply by being there when someone needs us, or saying the right words to set them on their path. I wrote this post after spending a really positive time with my young Gs. Sometimes it might seem like we have lost our way but rest assured, the youth are way more sussed than we give them credit for.

Newday
Despite what you read in the papers, the future is in safe hands. Just spent the last week with 7,000 courageous and inspiring young g's. Yeah there's work to do but don't ever get it twisted, the power of the youth will change the world for the better. I pray freedom, protection, good health, good education, good role models, safety, dignity, equality and peace for every single one of you. Love
(Instagram, 5 August 2018)

One of my favourite sayings comes from Ghana and it states that 'it takes a whole village to raise a child'.

I mentioned this saying once in an interview on Sky News, and the presenter took it quite literally saying, 'But we are not in a village in Ghana and people don't necessarily feel that there is much of a community, in some parts of London at least.'

What this African proverb actually means is that an entire community of people must interact with children in order for them to experience and grow in a safe and healthy environment. By *community*, I mean parents, siblings, neighbours, teachers, Government, police, youth services, all of these different groups coming together and saying, 'Okay, what can I do to improve the life chances of this child?'

I was blessed with having people like that in my childhood, revealing to me my purpose in life. If I had not been told I was a gifted writer in primary school, or had someone encourage me to write lyrics at an essential point in my teens, my life could have taken a completely different path. I'm not saying it *would* have done – there are a lot of ifs and buts – but there is a chance it *could* have.

Every young person needs someone to believe in them and to care about them. If I'd been given a selection of youth leaders and told to choose one, it is unlikely I would have picked Hafis as he was quite a lot older than me and didn't wear cool jeans or trainers – yeah, that mattered to me, remember. In fact, he wasn't cool at all. As it is, that man changed my life, and the reason he changed my life is because he cared about me. That is a perfect example of where one of my favourite sayings comes in handy: 'We don't care what you know; we just need to know you care.'

It was the same with Ms Aanonson. We had zero in common besides us both turning up to school each day – she was most probably a fan of Frank Sinatra or something – but she believed in me, and that was all I needed.

Actually, I should ask Ms Aanonson what music she likes as we have stayed in touch. I went back to my primary school after winning my MOBO in 2010, to talk to the school about my music, and she was there. She often gets in touch whenever she hears me on the radio or TV.

I wonder how many other people's lives she changed with one simple comment. I bet over the course of her career it's been loads. That is the sign of an amazing teacher.

When I was growing up, if I ever got into trouble close to home, my neighbours used to open up their front doors, stick their heads out and say, 'Isaac, you better behave yourself.' I listened to them because they were friends of my parents. They weren't my teachers or my mentors, but they were people who knew me, had watched me growing up and, on some level, cared about me. I never considered this at the time, but now I think about it, they offered me security. The reason they looked out for me was because they were adults and I was a child. Our roles were clearly defined.

Mazza is a slang term for madness. I noticed that things like serious youth violence were becoming the norm in youth culture and I believe that God has given me a voice to speak to the culture with an alternative message. For me, madness, or *mazza*, is to disrupt the norm – that's something that I want to do, because a young person taking away the life of another should *never* be normal. In today's culture, loving your neighbour or turning the other cheek can be seen as madness, but that is the madness that I want to see.

Mazza

Heard my man got snuffed.
No lie that could've been us.
God, please guide all those he loved.
When we feel down, man, we look up.
Gotta turn that pain to purpose.
Life too short, so we gotta merk it.
Still, make mistakes, but I'm learning.
These hands, they're made for workin',
But they told me I weren't good enough.
Still wouldn't give it up, God's got bigger stuff.

Lost my confidence, but had to pick it up, then I
    switched it up.
Now I'm confident,
Not cocky – and they can try and block me but they
    can't stop me,
Cah this is where God wants me.
So I might pull up to the spot and do a mazza.

I was in my yard when I heard two
Shots go off, them tings flew right past.
Mum had to move us out of the council block,
But we didn't move too far.
So I still saw goons on the corner setting up shop.
But I couldn't do that, darg
'Cos I saw dad wake up then work two jobs all for my
    future, yeah.
So I ain't got time for the messin'.
Pace ninety-nine like Fredericks.
Run up with the mic no guest list.
Make your head spin like Zepplin.
Got me back in the block, I'm investin',
Gotta get it for Steven Lawrence and Damilola.
The whole of the village be on a roller coaster.
Turn bloodshed into success and that's for the culture,
And they can try and block me, but they can't stop me,
Cah this is where God wants me.

Never went Eton, but still I battle on.
A tracksuit don't make me a vagabond.
For ten years I've been challengin'
Stereotypes, but I guess it's not a sprint, it's a marathon.
Still got the next flow and in
Death and grief still got the best hope.

It's do or die when they step on the roads.
They lose lives on their cellular phones, and then we
    go again.
So now we gotta get in the zone and
Build bridges, so the mandem can grow.
And all I know is when God says 'yes', no one can say
    'no'.
So put me to the test an' watch the boy go.
I hope my son knows
That they can try and block me, but they can't stop me,
Cah this is where God wants me.

Sometimes, if I'm in a shop buying something and I see a young boy there at the same time, I always try and nod at him because I want him to know that I have clocked him, that I have spotted the fact that he exists. It is my way of saying, 'Hello, we're both on this life journey together.' It's not much, but in that simple nod, I want to show that there is a distinction between that boy thinking the world is a kind, welcoming place in which he can be safe and grow, and thinking that the world is a hostile battleground.

So, that's what I mean by the proverb, 'It takes a village to raise a child.' All adults in society have a responsibility to take care of young people.

Does it always happen? Course not. I'm not naive enough to think that everyone gets a break, but I do believe that everyone deserves one and that it's up to adults and protectors to shine the light.

A few years ago, Danny, a friend of mine, committed suicide by jumping off a high-rise building in Canning Town. He wasn't a child; he was a young man just beginning to make his way in life. No one knows what the trigger was that led Danny to take his own life, perhaps it was a mental-health-related illness, or he felt helpless, or maybe he had got himself into some sort of trouble. Whatever it was, we had no idea that he was living so close to the edge, as he was always the life and soul in any setting. What is so tragic is that he was loved, truly loved, and I don't think he realized how loved he was. He had a young son, and family and friends. The problem with depression is that you feel like you are a burden to the world, that your sadness will bring other people down, which is why you can't talk about your pain, especially when the image you normally put out there is an upbeat one. If only Danny had found it in him to open up to other people about how he was feeling, he would have seen that the love was there, and maybe it would have saved him.

I want everyone reading this book today to know that they are valued and loved. This might sound simplistic, but through my faith, I believe that every single person is on this earth for a God-given reason. It might not be clear yet what that reason is, it might be staring you in the face and you can't see it, or like me, you might need someone to point it out to you – but it's there. People often say to me, 'It's okay for you, Isaac, you've got your faith. You have got God guiding you.'

That is true. I believe that my path is steered by God, and that God lies at the heart of everything I do, but people find faith in all sorts. Your faith can be in your football team, your family, your work, or anything in which you find inner strength. Just dig around and locate what you believe in or, if this is not obvious, start reading into subjects, find an interest or a passion, and draw positivity and drive from that. Apply it to everyday life and you will find that by having focus and awareness, a positive place to navigate your energy, you will at least start moving in a more positive direction.

11. SMALL STEPS

The reason I wanted to write this book, *Unspoken: Toxic Masculinity and how I faced the Man within the Man*, is because I realized that, for many years, a lot of the man within me was hiding away, too shy to reveal himself, or perhaps I was too reluctant to locate him. Yes, that was more likely. For most of my life, I was reluctant to dig deep in case I chanced upon unwanted hints of vulnerability. That would have been *bad*. Strong, independent, eldest-son-who-never-cries Isaac did not have a shred of vulnerability.

Solid as a rock.

This ingrained sense of masculinity led me to believe that the only emotion permissible for me to reveal was rage. I could be angry, upset, hurt, or sad and then punch something, because that is what men did. Bare my teeth. Tighten my fist. Either that or grin and bear it. Handle it. Withstand the pain.

I'm not a youth expert, psychologist, or professional youth worker, and I'm only at the start of my own parenting journey, but having lurched and swayed through the last few years of my life, one thing I am certain of is that 'Houston, we have a problem'. The hard-and-fast rules by which men are expected to live their lives scare me.

There, I've admitted it – I'm scared of the destructive

influence of masculinity. When young men draw knives and butcher one another, it is because they are living up to society's expectation of what men do – men fight.

However, a large number of the people knifing each other to death on the streets are not fully formed men; they are teenagers playing out what their fathers, uncles, brothers, musicians, actors, advertisers, world leaders *expect* them to be.

This alone is a big issue for our society, and when masculine toxicity manifests as fatal violence among young people playing at 'rage', it becomes a massive problem.

I hear a lot of talk about the 'crabs in a bucket' mentality among young people; that is, pulling each other down because of jealousy, hate, and limited opportunities. I think too much focus is placed on the *crabs* and not enough on the *bucket*. If the environment these people grow up in enables them to thrive, then there's no way they'll fight each other over scraps.

I want to show young people that the tight chains of conditioning can be undone. They are not set in stone.

I know this first-hand, because it used to be me. Now I am a free man.

Am I better for it?

Definitely.

I care deeply about young people reaching their full potential and when I say *potential*, I mean their physical, mental, and emotional potential. Provide someone with love, self-belief, self-awareness, and opportunities, and *boom!* The sky is the limit.

There are amazing people in this world doing amazing things to help young people make a start in life but, at the same time, there are a lot of bad decisions being made, which have a deep impact. On many levels, the 'village' is on fire. Young people are crying out for help, but their calls are being misinterpreted.

Human beings are not inherently bad: a teenager carrying a knife that kills another teenager is identified as 'a criminal', whereas in reality, nine times out of ten, that young person is a misguided child. People are not born with bad morals; we learn morals in early childhood from the primary people in our lives. How the people closest to us view the world, and our place in it, is how we come to view the world and our role in it.

If we are brought up to break the law, we are more likely to break the law. If we are brought up surrounded by people turning to violence as their default, we are more likely to turn to violence as our default. Equally, if we are brought up to respect the law and respect other people, this is most likely going to be the direction in which our moral compass is pointed.

Take elephants again: elephants, like humans, are naturally sociable creatures that rely on the bonds they forge within their extended family units, to navigate their passage through life. Older elephants guide the younger elephants in how to behave. When older elephants are poached for their tusks (sadly, a common occurrence), young elephants are orphaned, all of a sudden lost and alone without any clue where to turn and how to move forward. Without those in charge leading the way, they lose all sense of what is right and wrong, and default to running wild, attacking each other, and failing to form the necessary close relationships, resulting in a whole load of maladjusted, orphaned elephants.

And it isn't that different on our streets.

In order to build a fully functioning society, it is the

responsibility of the adults to behave as protectors, steering children in the right direction, and that means the whole 'village', from those in charge of the loot right down to those waving an authoritative finger at the kids messing about outside their front window. When the adults fail, the young lose their way.

> We need to restore faith, hope, love, and ambition to young people. Every young person needs to know that whatever your background, upbringing, race, age, gender, you can achieve some great things in this life. Before the older generation criticizes the young, remember who raised them ;)
> #DoYouDoYourJob
> (Instagram, 26 May 2014)

The problems we have don't begin with kids slaughtering each other on our streets – this is the point we arrive at when we have taken a million wrong turns. As adults, we need to turn the mirror on ourselves and ask: How have we reached this point? How have we failed these young people to the extent they are turning to violence? Which bit of our broken society are *we* responsible for? And most importantly, what can I/we do, to get these young people's lives on track?

> The problem with youth violence is that there isn't just one problem, and when there isn't just one problem, it means there isn't just one solution. One of my teachers used to say, if you point the finger at someone, you've got 3 pointing back at yourself.
> If you don't care enough about it then that's cool, do you my g. But if we all want to see the hood become a better place, and we all want to stop

seeing young lives being lost so easily without a care in the world, then we ALL need to take some ownership.

That goes for privileged and out of touch government officials that have never stepped foot in the ends, cowardly feds that stereotype young people and use unnecessary force for no apparent reason, and influencers who can encourage their fans / followers to make better choices in life.
(Instagram, 11 April 2018)

Government funding + improved housing + employment + education + opportunity + empowerment + safeguarding + mentoring + counselling + youth support + parents + neighbours= happy, well-adjusted kids.

With the Government's austerity cuts – with further cuts likely at the time of writing, following the Covid-19 pandemic – council budgets have been slashed by fifty per cent, which has had a direct effect on the poorest people in society as they are the ones most reliant on council services to support them.

The Government consists largely of white men over the age of fifty, privately educated, unworldly, and privileged, who are in charge of putting a fat red line through funds allocated to services that *prevent* youth crime, while adding in a whole new line dealing only with the fallout of crimes when they occur.

This brings to mind one of my favourite quotes attributed to Albert Einstein: 'Everybody is a genius, but if you judge a fish by its ability to climb a tree, it will live its whole life believing it's stupid.'

Einstein nailed it! We're only as good as what we know.

To get society fully functioning, we need the decision-makers in the House of Commons and the boardrooms to be made up of the young, old, black, Asian, white, male, female, rich, middle-class, and poor – from every walk of life, and from a wide range of professions, top-down to bottom-up. They not only need to come together, but also need to work together to identify all the necessary components and place them in a logical order of importance.

Until we combine wealth of experience, insight, and knowledge with common sense and adequate funding, we are letting our young people down.

When teenage homicide escalates and hits the headlines, there is a lot of talk, as well as promises and knee-jerk reaction from Government and relevant institutions to 'make Britain safe' and 'rescue a dying generation'. But once the coverage has died down, so does the interest. Life goes on. Only a small handful of government officials have ever ventured voluntarily into inner-city areas to talk to local people about the root causes of youth crime, away from the cameras and under the radar.

If ever the spotlight is on the issues, you can be sure that there's a political campaign attached.

Easy Road

We can't really complain,
But I still got a lot to say.
Looking for a way to stop the chain
Of events, couple feds said we'd be locked away
By the age of 16, so I stopped to pray.
I guess we had to flock to faith,

Cos aint no hand-outs that standout, well not
    today, man.
And my daddy couldn't top the pain, fam.
He packed his bags and he got the plane, ran.
And they wonder why we're jumping over barriers
    for trains
And were underachieving in every way, that's cos I
    never been raised.
What do you expect, I'm just running my race?
The only way I know how try and get the lowdown cos
I can't relate to all these suit-wearing politicians.
Yeah they been private school, but haven't got the
    wisdom.
They've never stepped foot on my estate. If they did,
    then I would stop to listen.
I'm just surrounded by flick knives and sick crime.
They did time and came out, went back in.
That's real life. I live like my brain down,
But no more I'm so sure.
I found faith, I'm on board.
Was down low, now Concorde.
So slow down, man, what for.

In the current epidemic of youth violence, knife crime is up
seventy per cent, with 1,012 knife-related hospital admissions
for ten to nineteen-year-olds recorded in 2019, compared to
656 in 2012/13 (NHS England). Many people think the problem
is only in London, but that is not the case; the problem is
countrywide, with a 47.5 per cent increase in knife-related
offences in thirty-four counties of England and Wales since
2010, versus an eleven per cent increase in London.

In 2017–18, Kent recorded the highest rise, with a 152 per
cent increase. Along with London and Kent, Nottingham,

Blackpool, Manchester, Slough, and Liverpool are now classed as some of the most dangerous places to live when it comes to youth violence (House of Commons Home Affairs Committee, 18 July 2019).

What's going wrong? The answer depends on who you ask. Those looking to divert the blame away from themselves will point the finger at the disempowered, misunderstood, misrepresented; at those attempting to whittle their way out of the life they have been assigned; namely, the perceived root of evil – drill and grime music artists.

Ask the police, the media, or authority figures at the top and they will say that it's drill and grime that are 100 per cent responsible for the recent increases in youth violence.

I'm not saying that it doesn't happen – in fact, I have proof that it does on very rare occasions. In the sixth form, I was sitting in English next to my best mate, Nick Brewer, when he got word that one of his close friends – the music producer Richie Holmes – had been shot and killed. The reason for the shooting? Richie had affiliated himself with an upcoming grime star, who had released a record insulting the perpetrator's half-brother.

A clear-cut case: music = murder.

And there are other instances where you hear about postcode wars being played out through the lyrics of drill music, and murders occurring as a result. There are people out there making money at the cost of someone else's pain. I know rappers, who were relatively unknown, who have been propelled to fame overnight by adding in a few lyrics of 'raw' and 'real' experiences of life at street level. If a particular music track is popular, it is going to get played all over the radio. Often the radio station doesn't know what the lyrics they are playing mean, or the damage they can do.

So, yeah, it does happen that certain tracks incite

violence and have repercussions, but these only represent a handful of people, although they give the whole urban music scene a bad name.

At the end of the day, anyone blaming music as the sole reason for these problems is failing to address their real root causes. It's cowardly.

Drill and grime music are the forms artists take to express the story of their lives as they see them. That is why there is a focus on drugs, money, status, tit-for-tat killings, and violence, as that is often their reality.

They could write positive lyrics focusing on hope, peace, and love, but when young people are lost, lack role models, and are looking for guidance to make sense of their world, they are more than likely to tune into the music that feeds into the negativity that exists in their own lives.

Those lacking power kick back through music. If their reality included secure and happy home lives, bountiful opportunities, and money and respect then that would be reflected in what they chose to put out. The negative themes in drill and grime aren't the *cause* of violent youth crime, but the *by-product* of the burning village.

Improve the outlook and the life chances of kids from the top down, give them something to hope for and believe in, keep them safe, and the message coming out will improve.

If we focus only on the negative aspects of drill and grime, we will fail to see the positivity it brings. Music of any kind creates opportunity where there may be no other possibilities, and enables expressive communication where there may be no other outlet. For many young people, seeing artists who look like them succeed in the music world spurs them on to be creative themselves. It shows them a way out. A large number of black music artists come from humble beginnings, and often grew up in the same neighbourhoods as the people who listen to their music – and they make it big, which offers young people hope.

When I was growing up there were a whole load of artists that I used to listen to, from all parts of the world, but the one that had the most direct influence on kick-starting me on my journey was Kano, because Kano grew up only fifteen minutes from my house, so had had the same kind of upbringing as me. But he'd made it onto MTV Base and, at the time, had just signed a major record deal.

That was huge for me. I remember I memorized all the lyrics to 'Ps and Qs', as a way of learning about the way lyrics are formed, and this was the launchpad for me to start writing on my own.

A few years later, I got the chance to meet Kano. I've met him a couple of times now, but the first time I went up to him, I told him what a massive influence he had been in my life. He is, like me, a man of few words, but appreciated it.

I often think it would make a big difference if those in authority tuned into drill and grime and got a sense of what life is like at street level. The lyrics reflect the mood, the difficulties, the frustrations, the lack of outlook, and aspirations. If those with the power to enact change took the time to listen, I reckon they could gain a lot of insight into the concerns young people have. Also, I'm not sure if they realize it, but many of their own kids are well and truly immersed in those genres of music, so it's funny when they're quick to condemn what their own kids are championing. Perhaps they don't mind as they can make sure their own kids aren't living the life – they're just taking musical enjoyment from other people's reality.

When I started out, I wrote negative lyrics relating to crime, money, sex, and drugs because I thought that was what rap was. I had no positive examples to inspire me. After losing a couple of friends, I stopped going in this direction, as sensationalizing someone else's reality no longer sat comfortably with me. I decided that what mattered was injecting hope into the reality I lived in, highlighting the changes I wanted to see. I started putting out positive messages, revealing the raw facts, but showing the other side of the coin – 'It doesn't have to be like this'.

I am not a fan of music that condones violence in any form. Sonically, of course it's enjoyable, but I try to veer from it where possible. It is true though that selling music is big business and despite the lip service that many artists pay to bringing peace to the streets, the money to be made from record sales has a way of outweighing goodwill.

It's not like that for everyone. There are a lot of artists who, like me, go against the grain, such as Akala, Novelist, and Nick Brewer. Every year, I take Allo Mate Live – a music event championing positive music – to the Rich Mix Arts Centre, in Shoreditch. Year on year, the event gets bigger and better, as more people understand the power of music to provide a fresh outlook. The negativity narrative is wearing, it brings you down, so sometimes people need to know that there is hope. Stopping the negative messages in rap music is not going to happen overnight, but while they exist, there needs to be another option.

Drill, grime, and rap are channels of communication that feed directly into the heart of communities that often feel most ignored. With the Covid-19 pandemic, the demographics most affected have been BAME (Black, Asian, and Minority Ethnic), inner-city, and working-class people. Rap has been quick to respond to the needs of these communities by promoting lyrics with a socially responsible message about keeping your distance and washing hands; direct communication that has much more sway with BAME listeners than 100 health messages put out by the Government.

So, although music might play a part in triggering violence, it also plays a far bigger role in enabling young people to make sense of their world and their place in it.

A more wide-reaching issue for youth violence than music is kids hanging around on the streets without anything positive to do, which I view as a sure one-way route to trouble. I see the closure of youth clubs and youth services as a far more pressing root cause. When I was growing up, youth clubs were alive and kicking, and largely responsible for keeping me out of trouble, finding my purpose, and putting it into practice. These places were where young people went to let their hair down, meet friends, make friends, find shared interests out of school, and hook up with positive role models.

Research conducted by the YMCA youth charity found that spending by local authorities on youth services decreased from £1.4 billion in 2010 to under £429 million in 2018–19, leading to the loss of 750 youth clubs and 4,500 youth workers up and down the country.

The closure of youth clubs forced young people onto the streets without anything specific to do, or anywhere specific to go, which increased the risk of them getting into trouble, falling into bad company, and become directionless. It's no surprise that the areas that have suffered the biggest cuts in youth spending are the areas that are now experiencing the highest levels of knife crime.

Youth Clubs play a vital role in young people's lives, particularly when the clubs are large enough to accommodate a lot of kids. Around 100 kids used to attend my youth club – that is a lot of kids staying off the streets.

In areas where poverty is high and home environments unsettled, youth clubs really come into their own. This type of set-up is common in boroughs where violence is rife and is a huge issue for young people. Young people need to feel love from day one of their lives and for it to continue consistently. Boys, in particular, rely on a father, or a strong father figure, for their social and emotional development. If they lack a close attachment to a male figure in their own world, they widen the net and start looking further afield among friends, social media, TV, music, or youth clubs for someone to emulate. Who they choose – whether a positive or negative role model – can determine the road they go down.

The sad truth, given a lack of youth services and positive distractions, is that the most likely road is usually the easiest road – the one that offers the greatest sense of belonging – which often centres on money, status, and drugs, as all of these serve to fill the void in their lives. I wrote about the influence of peers in 'Dun All the Hype':

Dun All the Hype

I got bros in jail.
Dem man won't get bail.
Forgive their sins.
Life ain't fairytales.
I got bro's in the grave.
That's real. The road ain't safe.
Forgive their sins
Hope that we see change.
I'm so focused now.
All I wanna do is make Dad proud.
Charles' son, Vivian's one.
Bars they come, Can't put the pad down.
There's bare madness ina my town.
Last week two man got gunned down.

This week three man just got found.
Next week four man might go down.
Got bro's in the bando,
Plotting and shotting them O's for the bankroll.
No Gucci, they got a gang though.
That's you G, me different angle.

Almost every debate and discussion on youth crime centres on the need to increase police numbers, come down hard on offenders, up the frequency of stop and search, issue gagging orders on drill artists, and dish out harsher penalties.

None of this sits well with me.

As a man of faith, I am all for turning the other cheek and practising forgiveness and tolerance in most aspects of my life, but as a black man, born and bred in London, I've got my issues with the police.

I am pretty certain that what I am about to tell you will resonate with many young black men living in the city, as it is pretty much standard, everyday practice.

A few years ago, I was shooting a music video with some friends for my single, 'Free'. This was two weeks after the unlawful shooting of twenty-nine-year-old Mark Duggan, in Tottenham, and so the atmosphere in London was more tense than usual. We were relocating from one part of London to another, and so packed the boot of my friend's Mercedes convertible with the filming equipment, with one of the items being a tripod stored in a long, black bag.

We had been driving for around five minutes when we noticed we were being tailed by an unmarked van. As we turned a corner, the van suddenly overtook us and eight armed police officers jumped out. Pointing their guns at the car windows, they told us to get out with our hands above our heads. When we were on the pavement, they threw us up against a wall. Some of them searched us, while the others searched the boot of the car. When we asked what they were doing they replied, 'You were spotted putting a gun in your car'.

Of course, all we had was the filming equipment. When they realized this, they lowered their weapons and said, 'Okay, you can go.'

That was it. No further explanation. No apology.

I was really angry about the way we'd been treated and so wrote a letter of complaint to the Independent Police Complaints Committee (IPCC), who issued me with an official apology.

I'm old enough and mature enough not to have an attitude of hate towards the police, but I completely understand why they are disliked, particularly by black people, as despite efforts over the years, systemic racism is still rife within the police force.

When it comes to something as inhumane as children knifing children to death, nobody wants to think of it as happening 'in their backyard' and so they distance themselves by stereotyping the perpetrators as deprived, fatherless, excluded, drug-fuelled black criminals, who deserve to die – a myth driven by misleading police statistics and attention-grabbing news headlines.

These are the inherent beliefs I want to challenge.

The reason we are not addressing the situation with any sense of urgency is because being perceived as a black or an ethnic-minority problem means that it is not afforded the same level of attention or investment as it would if the problem was perceived as 'British' or 'white'.

The reality is that when it comes to youth violence, it is

not a black-on-black problem. According to a year-long investigation, *Beyond the Blade,* conducted by the *Guardian* in 2018 into the impacts of knife crime on young people, the overwhelming majority of knife-related homicides committed over the last forty years were by *white* people living in densely packed *white* areas. 'Black-on-black violence' is a common term, but you never hear about 'white-on-white violence'.

The fact that the majority of knife crimes reported are 'black-on-black' is due to the police possibly skewing the facts, with the aim of justifying their racial-profiling agenda of stop and search. The term 'black-on-black crime' doesn't even make sense in my opinion. Black people don't kill other black people because they're black.

Despite the higher number of white incidents, nine times more black men are likely to be stopped and searched in comparison to their white counterparts. Black men are three times more likely to be arrested and three times more likely to be Tasered, and prison sentences for black people are harsher (Stopwatch Coalition).

Much of the problem lies in the way youth violence is perceived and reported, when the truth is that it's not exclusive to any *one* type of person from *one* type of background. It can include any young person from anywhere, who makes the 'mistake' of hooking up with a bad crowd. In almost all of the cases of knife crime highlighted in *Beyond the Blade*, the reasons for committing knife offences stemmed from deep-rooted problems relating to mental health, unemployment, poverty, or exclusion from school – aka, the 'burning village'.

Many years of harmful, misleading policing means that too many young black men have been criminalized unnecessarily. Police manhandling of black people has become so commonplace it is rarely questioned any more within the wider community. The question is never: 'Why is that policeman treating him like that?' but more likely to be, 'What has that black man done (now)?'

On 25 May 2020, the murder of George Floyd at the hands of police in Minneapolis, Minnesota, cast attention on the unlawful, unjustified killing of black people. The response was overwhelming, with people across the globe taking to the streets to protest. That was big, and it was powerful. Whether the support can be sustained and whether it will warrant any great change, is yet to be seen.

The social commentator Verna Myers refers to unconscious bias as a way of explaining institutional racism in police forces. She touched on this in her Ted Talk on this topic in November 2014, which attracted almost 1.2 million views:

> Police officers are deeply ingrained with erroneous ideas about who's dangerous. Looking at pictures of black kids, they're adding four years to their age, and are told that 'black people are crazy strong and have crazy [levels of] pain tolerance'.

The same can be said for the sub-music genres mentioned earlier: drill is driven largely by black artists and so is perceived to be more violent, dangerous, and criminal. Punk and heavy-metal lyrics used to have equally brutal undertones, but because these were largely the domain of white people, it was more relatable and so less feared.

This same level of unconscious bias is filtered through the whole of society and influenced largely by the way that black people are represented in film, TV, and music.

Recently, Emma and me were talking about how many times we'd each been stopped by the police. This particular discussion was interesting because we realized that, even though we'd both grown up in fairly similar, culturally diverse, and overpopulated areas of London, I had been stopped in my car more than fifteen times. And her? Zero. But when it comes to actual crimes committed, we're equal: none.

So why is it that she's never been stopped and I regularly have been? Unconscious bias. Whenever the police have stopped me, it's always been because they're randomly stopping vehicles to check they're insured, or because they're looking for someone that matches my description. It's a wonder that Emma has never been a victim of these 'random' stops, and strange that she's never matched the description of a wanted criminal before.

The problem with the *unconscious* aspect of the bias is that half the time, due to their conditioning, people don't even clock that they are behaving like this.

I told you earlier how I like to nod at youths to reassure them and offer them encouragement. I'm the same when it comes to the wider community. I consider myself a friendly person. I like to smile. It was after a trip to New York, where everyone is super friendly, that I came up with the idea for my clothing brand, Allo Mate. In New York, strangers greet one another in the subway, 'Hey, how you doin'?' I tried this on the Tube in London: 'Allo, mate,' but people steered away from me like I was unhinged. That was when I thought, *Hmmm, we need to fix this.*

I like people to feel that I am a positive presence in their lives, but I am aware of a high degree of unconscious bias. I sometimes wonder if it is because of this awareness that I do use such a friendly approach, as it's my way of trying to break down (unconscious) negative stereotypes.

Smile = black men are not to be feared.

It's as if I see my role as taking on people's biases single-handedly and resetting them on the right track.

I am a black man of African origin married to a white British person with a mixed-race son. I live in a predominantly white area, but grew up surrounded by people of different races and backgrounds, and I consider myself an open-minded, socially sound human being, yet I am still aware of people 'fearing' me because that is how I have been conditioned.

The truth is, I would love to be less apologetic about who I am. If I was a white man, would I still feel the need to smile at people?

Unconscious bias cuts deep and affects all of us.

Unless the police are prepared to build trust, train away their unconscious bias, and patrol positively, then they need to step back from the inner cities and leave the 'policing' to the protectors – that is, the members of the 'village' with young people's best interests at heart.

When knife crime is reported on the news, it is normally because the victim has been fatally wounded. What is less widely featured are the thousands of young people who end up in hospital each year with life-altering lacerations, multiple organ injuries, and loss of limbs as a consequence of being either stabbed or on the receiving end of a bullet. Media reporting places gang leaders and gang warfare at the heart of the problem, when as many times as not, desensitized young kids from dysfunctional homes are desperate for a bit of fame and glory and are messing about, without any concept of the damage that their actions might do to innocent lives.

The majority of youth crime is a senseless act of violence

by 'boys being boys', in the wrong place at the wrong time, living in the 'wrong' postcode, including disputes over phone chargers, girls, and video games; dares, blackmails and bribes. If a person carries a knife, they are three times more likely to be stabbed themselves.

In almost all the cases, brandishing a knife is an opportunity for young people to 'show off', gain points, prove they're gangster, win respect, and hide their inner fear and helplessness – that is, masculine toxicity ragin'.

As I mentioned before, showing any kind of emotion, or remorse or fear for your life doubles the danger: be tough or die.

The fifteen-year-old wielding the knife that kills the fourteen-year-old on the street, is he a criminal?

He must be if he's taken someone else's life.

Lock him up and throw away the key.

End of.

Except ...

What if ... the fifteen-year-old wielding the knife comes from a deprived, unsettled home, with a violent mother and an absent father, and is someone that finds his release at school, where he utters his cry for help through anger and aggression.

What if the school, unable to handle his emotional needs with their zero-tolerance policy, doesn't have the time, funds, or inclination to nurture him, so decides that permanent exclusion is the *right* course of action?

With nowhere to go, the fifteen-year-old is hanging around the streets and falls prey to a bad crowd that gives him friendship, confidence, and the offer of independent means in the form of £1,000 if he settles a dispute with an enemy crew. He is told that if he doesn't go through with the deed, he or a member of his family will experience the sharp end of the blade. He wants the money, although he doesn't want to hurt anyone, but he's too scared to admit it and so he goes along with it, acting the gangster. These people know where he lives. He has no choice. He wants to be respected, he needs some cash, he can see no way out.

And so he does what he is told and stabs a fourteen-year-old girl, kills her, and is locked away for twenty years, marked as a master criminal, a blight on our streets

When all he wanted was someone to care about him.

That is the reality for a lot of underage perpetrators. They are not inherently evil. They are not even very bad or slightly bad, they are just lost and disillusioned, and lack any other options.

In 2017/18, seventy per cent more young people were permanently excluded from school than in 2012/13, and forty per cent of prisoners had been permanently excluded from school (*Guardian*, 25 October 2019). As boys tend to externalize their mental-health problems through outward forms of aggression, they are more likely to be excluded than girls, who tend to keep a lower profile by withdrawing. So we could say that permanent exclusion is a way of discriminating against boys. But not *all* boys: black boys primarily, as they are three times more likely to be excluded from school than their white counterparts (Gov.uk).

Without youth services on hand to offer a safety net, or specialists in place to identify and offer the relevant mental-health support, young people with emotional needs, lacking any other obvious opportunities, opt to commit senseless acts of violence that put their own lives, and the lives of others, in danger.

There is no denying the pivotal role of parents in a young person's life. If it had not been for my own parents' strict rules and unfaltering love, I might be a completely different person from the one I am today.

We are told that the role of parents is to love their children unconditionally, and while this is the case and the intention 99.9 per cent of the time, things can go wrong. Life is not a fairytale. Families break up, poverty dictates lifestyle, mental health problems creep in, addiction plays a part, fathers leave, parents die, kids feel abandoned, discipline falls by the wayside ... If parenting was a guaranteed smooth ride there would not be hundreds of books giving advice on how to do it.

Although there is no denying that inadequate parenting is one of the reasons why young people might turn to violence and crime, it is not always inevitable. A few years ago, there was a stabbing in my area by a set of twins, both of whom were friends of mine. They were hauled up for beating a guy to death with a pole. The guy who died also happened to be a friend of mine.

The reason: an outstanding debt. As always, a simple issue that communication could have fixed, but which instead was overinflated due to masculine bravado. Where this tragedy varies from the majority is that the twins came from a good, loving, solid home: mum and dad both present; a lot of discipline and care. There was nothing obvious in their early lives to indicate what was to come.

As a society we are quick to blame the parents – again, it's easy and diverts attention from the rest of the village – but in this instance, it was not their home life, but the consequence of a toxic society that corrupted the twins.

When children get into bad company and become distant or out of control, parents worry, but often, they have nowhere to turn to voice their concerns. If they go to the police, their child will be labelled a criminal; if they go to Social Services, they are at risk of having their child taken away. They can't speak to the school if the child has been excluded, and friends and neighbours judge, and so, without the necessary support, it is down to a wing and a prayer that their child avoids getting into trouble of the ultimate kind.

I am not an expert on youth, but I want to play a role in young people's lives. That is why I go into schools, churches, and youth clubs to tell my story, so that people can see that for someone from the same beginning as them, there is another way to live. I have also joined up with the charity Power the Fight, which works at street level with families, churches, faith groups and community organizations to engage on issues relating to youth violence. The charity educates, invests in, and supports families who are first-hand victims of violence, and provides them with ways of getting their children back on track. There are amazing people doing amazing things, and many of these incredible people work at grass roots level, on the front line, dealing directly with perpetrators and victims of violence.

If we want the next generation of kids to succeed in life – and by *succeed*, I don't mean earn money and find fame; I mean be fulfilled and well adjusted – then we need to give them the tools to dig deep, be true to their souls, to know that society is looking out for them, that opportunities abound, and to gain the knowledge that they can direct their own future. Only then will they feel *safe* enough to chuck away the knives and resolve conflict by way of communication, not aggression.

12. PURPOSE

You might have heard me mention the word 'purpose' once or twice. This is a word that I use a lot because I believe that this seven-letter word makes all the difference between personal fulfilment and erring down the wrong track. Purpose is what we spend pretty much most of our childhoods searching for. Most of our lives actually. Often, we don't know that this is what we are doing, as it is disguised under several layers. For example, young people will think that all that matters is fitting in and being part of a group, but within that group they are actually seeking their purpose. Are they the funny one, the brainy one, the crazy one, the leader? They are looking for their 'reason to exist' in that group. If we have purpose, we are necessary.

What makes me really sad is when I hear young victims, or witnesses of crime, saying stuff like, 'I most probably won't make it to twenty-five, and if I do, I'll be in prison'.

Is that how it sits for you, with your life choices *dead* or *banged-up*?

The feeling that life has no purpose is the kind of attitude that youth violence instils in young people, due to the fear it breeds and the negativity it creates.

If that is how you feel, I want to say that is not the *true* you speaking; that is the you that you have created as a form of self-defence; the one that says, 'If I don't look like I care about my life, it won't matter how it ends up playing out.' Or maybe you think like this because you are too terrified to consider other options. Sometimes, survivors of knife crime, or witnesses of violent offences, are so scared of stepping out of their own homes, or of running into the wrong people at the wrong time, that the option of death or prison can, in some skewed way, seem like a preferable option.

I remember a couple of years ago, at the end of one of my shows, a boy came up to me. He was in his mid-teens.

'Great show, Guvna,' he said. 'I love your music as it allows me to escape from my life.'

I was concerned to hear him talk about 'escaping', as he seemed too young to be looking for ways out. I asked him what was going on in his life and he told me that he was too scared to leave his house, as he didn't want to be lured into a gang that was hanging around on his estate. He knew that if he joined the gang he would end up in some kind of trouble, but at the same time, if he didn't join, he was putting his life at risk. He was trapped. It was Catch 22. I could tell that he was really scared about the danger facing him and I tried giving him advice, but the truth is, besides rehousing him, which was out of my control, there wasn't much I could do. He knew what side of the tracks he wanted to be on, but it was practical support he needed to achieve it.

The fact is that for many young people growing up with danger on the streets, it sometimes seems like luck of the draw whether or not they live safe or dangerously, or in reality, live or die. Course it shouldn't be like this. I used to mentor a young teenager who lived on a London estate and lived in fear after being stabbed. The perpetrator had been sent to prison for five years, but as he was popular, with a whole load of friends, there was a lot of worry about my young kid's safety. In the end, the police, in partnership with Social Services, promised to rehouse him. That was three-and-a-half years ago and guess what – he's still waiting. The perpetrator is due out of prison in a little over a year and knows exactly where this boy lives. This youngster has been living in terror of his life while waiting for the authorities to follow through on their promise. It seems like they have let him down. What kind of message does that put out?

I hope that the experience of these young people is not your experience and that the reason you are reading this book is because you have every intention of living a long, rich, and fulfilled life, and that you feel safe, know you have a future ahead of you, and are simply in need of a little guidance as to how to get there.

When we are not equipped with the tools for locating our purpose – perhaps through living in an unsafe environment, being let down, or lack of visible opportunities – we are at risk of drifting blindly through life simply because we've got nothing in place to ground us.

I am often asked to speak in TV and radio debates on the topic of youth violence. Whenever I am asked how I 'got out', I answer that firstly, I was never really 'in', but what saved me essentially was finding my purpose.

When I was a young teenager without much clue of what I wanted to do with my life, and not much confidence in my abilities, I used to wake up in the morning, haul myself out of bed without much enthusiasm for the day ahead, drag myself to school, daydream through my lessons, waiting for break time when I could see my friends, hang around all evening watching TV or playing computer games, and then wake up the next day and repeat that same cycle.

Looking back at those days I see them as all blending into one as I coasted through my life.

It was finding my faith and opening up about the true me though my music that woke me up and gave me the incentive to jump out of bed and start my day. Okay, maybe not jump out of bed – that's never been my style – but start the day with a plan and a purpose, and that has pretty much been me ever since.

If I had not let God into my heart or found a calling through my music, I would definitely have been a candidate for crime because I wanted so much to fit in.

Some people are born *knowing*: they know from the first moment they hold a paintbrush, a microphone, or a spade what their purpose is, but the majority of us struggle. We are filled with doubt: 'I could do that, but he's better,' or, 'I tried that, but it didn't work out.' So much potential in life is lost through self-doubt, through fear of digging deep and finding the true you, and through lack of perseverance.

Anyone who has followed me for a while will know that some of the lyrics I have put out into the world should never have seen the light of day, lyrics that I am too embarrassed even to put in the pages of this book, but they didn't stop me from writing more and getting better at my life's work. When I made *Odd1Out* and it didn't reach the dizzy heights I was hoping for, I could have quit then and there, and assumed I was a lost cause at the end of the road, but I never did.

I tried again and again.

And that's how you do it.

Keep trying.

A couple of years ago, I was booked to do a gig in Birmingham. I had done the same gig in London and sold out the venue, but my Birmingham promoter was not very good. I arrived and got out on stage expecting around 500 people in the audience, but only ten showed up and they rattled around like marbles in a tin, which was really embarrassing. I did the concert the best I could, but all the way through I felt really bad and dejected. As I got into my car, I decided, *Right, that's it. I'm never coming back here again to humiliate myself.* But then I stopped and thought, *Why, Isaac? What is that going to prove?*

Driving away into the night, I came up with another plan: *Okay, so that was really bad, but I'm going to do it again, to prove to myself that I can. On the next album, I will return to Birmingham and I will perform to a sold-out venue.*

I was determined to make something good out of the experience, even though inside I was feeling pretty wrecked. I stuck with the plan and a couple years later I returned. When I walked out on stage, every square metre of the venue was packed. *That's more like it*, I thought. I put on a great show for the people of Birmingham, made all the better by knowing that I had persevered and not thrown in the towel at the first hint of failure.

If you know what your purpose is and can see a road map to achieve that purpose ahead of you, you are ten times more likely not to stray off the path or be side tracked by 'easy' distractions.

You might think I make the whole process of 'finding my purpose' sound easy. That is not the case. It took me years to figure out who I was and I'm still trying to figure a lot of it out now. But once I found my purpose, I committed to it and told myself that I had every right to do it and put everything I could into making it work.

Of course, it was made a whole lot easier by having

my youth leader beside me every step of the way, rooting for me, not letting me come off the path, and that is not necessarily going to be your story, but if you can find it in you to believe in yourself and tell yourself that you have as much chance as anyone else on Planet Earth of fulfilling your potential, then you will find your inner drive to succeed.

I take my position as a role model very seriously. It's not just a phrase I throw about when I feel like it. I know that as long as my heart is beating, I have the capacity to make a difference in people's lives, and my focus is mainly with young people. The future of every family, community, innovation, space journey, boardroom, or government office rests in the hands of the young. Get it right with the next generation, and we get it right for the future, as the American author and social reformer Frederick Douglass (1818–1895) stated: 'It's easier to build strong children than to repair broken men.'

For many years now, I have worked in a mentoring role for people in need of guidance and self-belief. My mentoring career started when I was still at university, when I joined up with the Eastside Young Leaders Academy and mentored secondary school kids with their homework, playing games, and doing team-building exercises. After university, I went freelance and started going into schools and delivering workshops on peer pressure and online bullying, and helping young people to find ways of fulfilling their potential. I must have visited over 100 schools in my time working with Year 7s up to sixth formers. Mentoring is about building relationships of trust with young people, offering the kind of advice, support, and encouragement that I have received many times over the years.

I want other people to have significant people saying the

right stuff to them, at the right time, as I have had in my life. Success is not only about a four-bedroom house, nice car, and trainers; it is also about influencing and investing in young people. When I am an old man, sitting in that rocking chair, grandkids round my knees, I won't be reflecting on the money in the bank or the days spent carving up lyrics at my desk – I will be reflecting on the lives that I have changed and the people who have benefited from that change. That will be how I measure my success.

Children grow up much faster nowadays and, as a result of the influence of social media, the gap between children and their parents is growing much wider much earlier, often before kids are old enough to get a grip on how to handle themselves safely. This is when negative role models can creep in. In 2019, the National Crime Agency revealed that the child-exploitation industry was worth £500 million. Gang members, by way of Snapchat and Instagram, grant themselves celebrity-style influencer status, glamorizing the gang-life dream of riches and respect. They work by tapping into smartphones and coercing and blackmailing kids, to the extent that both they and their family are put in fear of their lives.

We live in a time where news is transmitted via social media faster than it takes to call an ambulance to a crime scene. Death is no longer a private event and this ups the stakes for young people and gets them more involved more quickly.

When I was growing up, if someone was beaten up by a rival group, there were no cameras filming it and so the event ended there and then a lot of the time. Now, it is all tied in with *respect*. The perpetrating group takes the upper hand by posting a video of the beaten-up victim, forcing the rival group to retaliate, but going one step further to rid themselves of the shame by raising the stakes from *fist* fight to *knife* fight. And so the deadly cycle of tit-for-tat killings begins.

I've known a few mentors who are not much older than the kids they mentor, who have been on the receiving end of violence, are now doing well materially, and understand the way kids speak, the world they come from, and the trials they are facing. When parents lose their way with their children, it can reach the point where they lose their ability to rein them in. This is scary for parents and for the young people as well, as sometimes they get in so deep, they can't find a safe way out. With mentoring, I sometimes bridge the gap between children and their parents, finding ways to bring them back together, not in a professional capacity like a social worker, but by getting them to realize that they are not the only ones in that situation, trying to show these kids that there is another way to live, and getting parents and kids to open up and talk together.

When you see a path laid out before you in life, it appears as a straight line. For me, the straight line was to write music, perform my music, make a living, build up a fan base, and become well known for what I do – a linear journey from A to B. It is only by setting out on the path that you realize there is so much more to take into account along the way. What I never imagined when I began chalking out my route were the pressures involved with being an award-winning musician, a role model to the many people experiencing the same start in life as me, living in the public eye, and being open to a whole array of judgement. For many years I struggled with 'growing up' in the open for all to see. If I made a mistake, it couldn't be brushed under the carpet.

Instead, it was stamped on my forehead: 'Gather round, one and all, Guvna B has stumbled.'

I used to feel the pressure not to mess up my responsibilities quite intensely, not to put out mixed messages to young people, and not to write music that was unrelatable. It mattered hugely to me that young people had a role model, and so I felt I had to be there for them, believe in something for them, act out my beliefs, shout out on their behalf, even when I didn't feel true to myself.

After my dad died, for a while all of those fears and distractions melted away. I suddenly saw myself for the human being I was, with all of the vulnerability I talked about earlier seeping in. That was the turning point for me to be myself; to be true; to lift the mask; and show the hurt, struggling, confused, lost, angry, sad, bewildered *me* beneath.

From that point on, my approach to my music and to my 'extended family' of fans has been to maintain that honesty. The same applies to my mentoring. When I mentor young people now my aim is to get them to lower their mask and reveal their true souls. This is very hard for a lot of people, especially as many of the young people come from troubled backgrounds, where violence predominates; from toxic homes, where to cry is to show weakness; or from situations where being true to who they are can get them murdered. Lowering the mask and revealing vulnerability enables them to take a step back and assess the world from a whole different point of view.

I am often asked to give advice to young people looking to start out writing songs. I used to think, *Woah! There's so much. Where do I begin?* But now I have done it a few times, the same piece of advice always pops to the surface first and that is because I view it as the most important thing: Be yourself. Don't try and be anyone but yourself.

The world already has a Guvna B; it doesn't need another. Laying yourself open for judgement is part and parcel of being creative. There are always going to be believers and doubters, but you need to switch off from the external noise, listen to your heart, and never be afraid of putting out something fresh. Some of the most honest, secure, and joyful people I have ever met were not in Britain, but in my travels around the world.

Let me tell you about the kids I met in Zambia

My wife Emma is always trying to get me to go on holiday.

'It's ages since we went away,' she said to me.

I replied: 'What? Look at my passport! And I showed her all the stamps of the countries I'd toured that year.

'Those aren't holidays, Isaac,' she said. 'Those stamps are for you turning up in a country, doing a sound check, performing your show, and coming home. Half the time you don't even know what country you're in.'

She had got a point there: a lot of my travelling involves whistle-stop tours. The way I get the *feel* of the country is through my audience and how they respond to the music. However, there was one trip I did, which was different from touring and different from a holiday, and that was when I went to Zambia.

I went as a volunteer for the international relief charity Tearfund. I've travelled to a few countries in Africa, Ghana being the one I've been to most of all obviously, to visit family and perform a bit. But this was my first time in Zambia.

I stayed in a city called Ndola, and it was sick. I went there hoping to tell young people my story and inspire them, but it was me who ended up being completely inspired. I sang a bit and gave a couple of talks, but most of my trip involved chatting to people, witnessing first-hand how they lived, hearing their stories, the issues that mattered to them, what they got up to in their free time. And the truth is that I floated about on their positivity.

I went to this one seventeen-year-old girl's house. She was studying to be a lawyer, but had recently bought some chickens and set up a business selling eggs in order to help support her family. She was really proud of her business, but to make it fully viable, she needed a generator which she didn't have, as she couldn't afford one.

I said, 'Come on, Tearfund, let me buy that generator.' I wanted to make a difference to her life, and it seemed such a simple act of kindness. The employees at Tearfund explained it to me though. They said, 'Isaac, throwing money at issues is just a quick-fix solution, when what you need to think about is the long term.'

I thought: *What? But it's just what she needs, and I can make a difference.*

I pictured her whole life changing as a consequence of that generator.

But I was wrong.

What I learnt from that trip is that charities don't go in and write up a long shopping list of stuff to buy, otherwise local people become dependent on them for all their needs. Instead, they use the funds they receive through donations to put structures in place to educate, create opportunities, and encourage self-sufficiency. Generators rust and run out of fuel, but skills are for life.

It was me all over again, growing up on my estate thinking that those Nike Air Max trainers were the root to all happiness, when they were really a quick-fix solution, a short-term spike. My true happiness came when I found my direction in life. The only way to break the cycle of poverty from one generation to the next, the hand-to-mouth existence worldwide, is to lay the foundations, plant the seeds, build partnerships, and enable people to grow.

What really struck me about my trip was that I was 7,000 miles from home but still discussing the same issues I discussed at home. I was moved by how similar we all are. Wherever and whoever we are, we all have the same hopes, fears, and outlooks. We all care about our loved ones, our day-to-day living, and finding our reason to be on this earth.

To give you a taster of what my trip to Zambia meant to me, take a look at this post:

> The thing I love the most about the young people I met in Zambia is the fact they are being the change they want to see. It's proper inspiring. I visited young people who had started their own businesses and a Junior Parliament who are effecting change. One of the things they did was campaign that a local hospital should have a generator which would provide light so women didn't have to give birth in the dark. (They were successful.) Not sure what your view of Zambia is, or Africa for that matter, but best believe that it is rich. Rich in people, rich in spirit, and rich in resources. Like any other country or continent there are challenges and we need to work together to see positive change. I'm looking forward to playing my part. Thankful to see the work that @tearfund do out there. Thank you Zambia … I've got a lot of love for your peaceful nation. P.S #AfricaIsNotACountry. (Instagram, 28 January 2019)

I hope this chapter, in a roundabout way, has shown you why

having a purpose in life gives you something to build on, keeps you focused, and provides you with the confidence to carve your own path. Don't go thinking I've got it all clear-cut in my head though. I'm still living and learning every day, and get a lot of my inspiration from Colossians 3: 23: 'Anything you do, work at it wholeheartedly as if working for the Lord and not for human masters.'

One thing I am sure of is that God wants me to help young people. That message is coming at me loud and clear.

How do I go about it though?

I used to spend a lot of time trying to figure out the 'how?' and waited for God to give me a sign, while finding the courage to be true to my convictions.

That is when I figured that there are two types of people in this world.

1. People who know why they are here;
2. People who let the world tell them.

I don't want the world to tell me. I spent a lot of my early teenage years having the world tell me that and it didn't feel good.

The Grammy award-winning American hip-hop artist Lecrae said: 'If you live for people's acceptance, you will die from their rejection.'

The world has a tendency to find fault in everything we do, so we need to be confident in who we are as people. It's very easy always to look left and right and say, 'That person is doing better than me,' or to judge yourself by the number of YouTube views or streams, or tickets sold. This is not how God views success. This is success seen through the eyes of humans and it will never bring personal happiness or joy.

Walking with God gives me peace; peace that if I don't

ever own a Lamborghini, I'll always be good, because God's got me, and I've still got a purpose in this world. And if I do ever get to own fancy stuff, they won't define me, because God defines me.

After spending time looking around for 'how' to fulfil my purpose and help young people, I realized that there isn't just one way, God wants me to try a whole load of things. That is why I go knocking on different doors and seeing what works. If God gives me a green light, I walk through. Now, I just work as hard as I can and hope that God blesses the work that I do. In the words of Saint Augustine: 'Pray as though everything depended on God. Work as though everything depended on you.'

Do I get rejections? Yes, all the time. Rejection is part of life – a vital part – and if used correctly, it motivates us to do better.

If rejection worries you, just remember that rejection was a big part of Jesus's life. He was even rejected by those closest to him, as quoted in John 7: 5 – 'For not even his brothers were believing in him' – but God put something in his heart, just like he has put something in your heart, and if God puts something there, whatever it might be, a passion, a need, a motivation, then it is meant to be there and something is meant to happen. You just need to believe in yourself and not hold back from trying new things in the hope that, by opening many doors, you will find your path.

13. BEYOND OUR CONTROL

'What do you most fear, Isaac?' For some reason people like to ask me this question, I've no idea why. Last time it happened I answered, 'Dying empty.' This came out without a hesitation.

Boom!

I didn't need to think of what to say, it was right there.

I suppose the reason the answer came so fast was because I had just released a new album, *Everywhere + Nowhere*, which was inspired by a photographer called Vivian Maier (1926–2009). You might have heard of her, but chances are, you haven't, and the reason I say this is because, for the eighty-three years that she was alive, no one *had* heard of her. Throughout the course of her life, she took around 100,000 photographs that depicted urban American life, but she hardly printed any of them.

The reason she was in my mind when I answered that question was because it was only after her death that she soared to fame, when a box of her undeveloped negatives was picked up at a local auction by a local historian, who decided to look into the story of her life. Her art is now celebrated worldwide, but it is too late for her to reap any of the rewards.

Vivian Maier's story really got me thinking. On the one hand, it seems to me that she did *die empty*, because although she found and fulfilled her purpose by taking thousands of photos and used her talents the best she could, she didn't achieve absolutely everything possible because she never got to see the impact her work had on the lives of other people.

A bittersweet triumph.

My album, *Everywhere + Nowhere*, is about bittersweet experiences, and explored the two extremes and how they are present in my life.

My son, Ezra, was born in September 2019. He inspired this freestyle.

Ezra's Freestyle

I just seen my mum turn Grandma,
Lil bro turn uncle Joey,
Wife turn baby mum.
Me, I turn homely.
Got a couple blessings at the crib.
Em that's my rib.
My son that's a king.
I just wish that my dad could see this.
This is legacy, sacrifice, all the feelings.
When he died, I thought, God, I don't deserve this.
But now I'm looking at my son thinking, God I don't
    deserve this.
Moral of the story: take the rough with the smooth,
Cos if it's all working together, I still win when I lose.
Every test is a lesson.
The lesson is a blessing.
Choose to see the message.

I got mine in my possession.
I know I said the last pic was the last pic,
But this a vid so the bars had to touch grid.
Gone for a bit cos I'm tryna be a Dada.
But when I come back just know it's gonna be a mazza.
Still feeding the raps,
But I'm gone cos my son needs a feed and a nap,
And a nappy change

That first day of his life I was so happy: I was a daddy, I had a baby boy, a wife as well, but then the sadness began to sink in at the thought that my dad would never get to meet his grandson. We were so happy to give Ezra the middle name Nii-Boye, which was my dad's Ghanaian name, meaning, 'first-born', but the happiness was tainted with sadness when I thought about how my dad had died before knowing that his legacy lived on in a whole new generation.

Picking up the keys to our new house was a happy day, but also sad, as my dad would never set foot inside it.

I told you before that when my dad died, I had a feeling of sitting beside him in the hospital, thinking that perhaps his purpose had been to leave behind everything he knew in Ghana, in order to find a new world in which to raise a family, see his sons grow up, happy and working hard ... If that was the case, then it was mission accomplished for my dad.

It wasn't the same for Daisy or Franklyn, as their time was cut short when they still had a whole lot more to give.

I miss them all and wish every day that they were still here, but the passing of these three significant people from my life has allowed me to open up, discover the man within, and find a whole new sense of purpose.

Bittersweet

Wha'g'wan, this is su'tt'in' like an update.
It's been one thousand-odd days, still I'm up late.
Wouldn't say it ever gets easy but I must say
A few more laughs of recent, but it's love hate,
'Cause, on the one hand, I'm thankful that I'm
      moving forward.
On other, I feel guilty last year
I bought a coffin and a house within a few months.
It's like I get a little joy and then I lose some.
Yeah.
Never thought I'd own a house before 30.
But never thought you wouldn't be around this early.
I was happen the day I picked up the keys,
Still got reluctant peace.
Everything's bittersweet.
Still got most of the gifts you've given me.
It's like they're keeping you close, never ghost.
Reminders all over the home. But better know
What I'd give for you to pick up the phone.
It's like you're everywhere and nowhere.
It's like you're everywhere and nowhere.
It's like you're everywhere and nowhere.
Feeling everything and nothing.
I'm just praying and I'm trusting.
Everywhere and nowhere.

God, I can't lie, our relationship was strained last year.
Couldn't handle the pain last year.
I thought the faith that I had was all in vain last year.
I thought the sun would never shine after the rain last
      year.

But I just stepped outside, it's kinda sunny,
With a westerly wind,
And I guess that's like the blessings You bring.
There's good times, hard times, and we wrestle
    within.
So now it's sweet chin music when I step in the ring.
It's a miracle I'm standing today.
And I wouldn't have made it if it wasn't for grace.
I know even in the darkest of days You never left me
    alone.
I remember I was calling Your name.
I wasn't getting an answer and I was getting
    frustrated,
And so I opened the Bible,
I started turning the pages,
And I read, You're keeping watch over the good and
    the evil.
I can't see You, but You see all Your people.
It's like You're everywhere and nowhere.

I don't know what the future holds,
But I know who holds the future.
So I'm good to go.
Had some highs and we had some lows.
My mother told me that You're with me,
And that's good to know.
I took it slow.
There's times and seasons,
And they shook the boat.
Hands are made for working,
That's the book I wrote.
Now I'm practising my preach.
Time to hit the road.

I've worked hard over the course of my career and now have a strong CV; my albums sell well; I'm supporting my family ... but the weird thing is, no matter how much I talk about self-confidence and finding purpose, and about success being measured only by the Man Upstairs, I still suffer from my own insecurity. The more that people perceive me as doing well, the less sure I am of my abilities.

It's like I feel driven to progress, which comes from my mum always telling me to be the best I can be, but equally, I am happy where I am, which is my dad saying, 'Cool cucumbers, son.'

Every time I do achieve something, I enter a new 'room' filled with people who appear bigger and better than me, which feeds my insecurity and causes me to start questioning my qualifications for being there in the first place.

My best friend, footballer Joe, sums it up well. Aged seventeen, he got a youth contract with West Ham and so he went and bought himself a nice car, a brand new Renault Clio, and everyone was like 'Woah, Joe! You've hit the big time.' It was the best car in school. Then he went up a level and began training with older players, who drove Mercedes, and with him in his Clio he was suddenly at the bottom of the pack. So, he bought himself a BMW, but then he progressed up to the next level and there were older players driving Bentleys. No matter how many rungs he climbed, there were always others ahead of him.

If you look at celebrities in magazines or on Instagram, they make out they are living the dream, happy in love, 24/7 partying, but none of them are resting easy. Even if they really are at the top of their game, they have to hang on tight, because they are all too aware that the higher the climb, the further the fall.

This is why, when the benchmark is set by human values, success is an illusion.

One of my biggest insecurities is that I call myself a musician, but the truth is that the only instrument I can play is the triangle. LOL! I had a go at the viola in school when the music teacher tried to get everyone to have a go at something, but because it wasn't *cool*, I quit. I regret that now. That's why I say to all young people, when your music teacher tells you to have a go: 'Don't quit, no matter how uncool you might perceive the instrument to be. Stick with it, because it might just be a route to finding something you're good at.'

Put me in a room full of real musicians and I instantly feel out of my depth. I remember how proud I was when 'Cast your Cares' was taken up as a worship song in church. I was asked to come and sing it live. So, I did. There I was at the sound check and the room was filled with all these big musicians and someone called out, 'Hey, Guvna, what key is it in?'

I was like, 'What?' I had to reveal my ignorance and that made me feel really inadequate.

Whenever I feel low or inadequate, or my impostor syndrome is attempting to chew me up or wear me down, I find ways around it by challenging myself to be better today than I was yesterday. I do this because I never want to feel like I am wasting the opportunities I have been given, and by giving into feelings of doubt and insecurity, I am letting myself, my parents, and all those who believe in me down.

This is why, when I tell young people to make the best of the tools they are equipped with, I mean it. Doing this myself stops me from making a list of all the stuff I *don't* have, while at the same time enabling me to open up the storage cabinet of everything I've got.

My favourite people to hang out with are kids and elderly people because they seem to not let their fears get the better of them. Kids haven't seen enough and elderly people have seen it all. They do anything and say anything without fear of being judged. The Vivian Maier photo I chose for the cover of *Everywhere + Nowhere* sums up exactly what I mean (picture 21). I bet the kids in that photo didn't have much in the way of material goods, but check out those smiles:

Reflecting about how it's only 5 days until my album's out. The album was inspired by the photographer, Vivian Maier. She spent her whole life taking pics but never got discovered until after her death.

This is one of her pics and it inspired the album cover. Just a bunch of kids having a good time in their community. If I was to guess, I'd say these kids probably didn't have it all but I love the joy in this pic.

I think a lot of us can relate. Might not have the desired family setup, enough money, and enough opportunities or the temptations, distractions, and hurdles of life might be tryna pull you back .... but big up everyone tryna count their blessings, smile through it, find joy and keep fighting through it all while putting one foot forward everyday.

Might not be where you wanna be, but thank God we ain't where we used to be. Life's a journey man. *Everywhere & Nowhere* out this Friday! Big love to everyone that has pre-ordered the album and grabbed the Merch too. I know this music is gonna bring a lot of hope
(Instagram, 29 March 2020)

I've chatted a fair bit with prisoners in the past on National Prison Radio and always found it enlightening. Again, stereotypes would have us believe that all prisoners are hardened criminals, but, often they are people caught up in the wrong place at the wrong time, with the wrong colour of skin, an inability to articulate, or are simply lost and looking for someone to care.

Although I believe that, where due, adequate punishment is really important, I am particularly passionate about rehabilitation for children and young adults. Research shows that young adults aged eighteen to twenty-four have brains more closely aligned with children than with older adults, with the parts of the brain responsible for maturity being the last to develop. This is the part of the brain responsible for weighing up long-term costs versus short-term gains, which impacts on a person's ability to show empathy, remorse, and foresight.

Writing young people off as criminals does not take into account the massive strides they make when their brains do reach maturity, which is usually not until they are in their mid-twenties and better able to get a better grip of cause and effect. This is why rehabilitation as a key to prison reform is a far more positive way of helping young people turn their lives around, than harsh, often debilitating punishments.

Had the privilege of sharing my story and talking about youth culture on National Prison Radio today. Broadcasted across 109 prisons up and down the UK – I was interviewed by Daryl, one of the inmates who has a keen interest in Radio. I think it's sick that he isn't letting his mistakes keep his mind locked up. Everyday we can improve, believe, and achieve more. Got to play my song Fairytales too which I wrote for my friends in jail and those who have passed away. 'I got bro's in jail, them man wont get bail. Forgive their sins, life ain't fairytales. I got bro's in the grave, that's real, the road ain't safe. Forgive their sins, hope that we see change.' So much potential in young people and it's important to do all we can to make sure it's not wasted. (Instagram, 28 May 2019)

Knowing that there is someone in the world caring about you and believing in you, makes all the difference to the way we conduct ourselves. It gives us a reason to be. Being locked up in prison is a massively isolating experience. It is very easy to feel like the world outside is carrying on as normal and has forgotten all about you. I know it has been particularly bad during the Covid-19 pandemic when, owing to social-distancing measures, families were forbidden from visiting, and inmates told to stay in their rooms for twenty-three hours a day. This was why, when I was asked by National Prison Radio to help with prisoner morale, by recording a sixty-second message showing the inmates that the outside world was still thinking about them, I jumped at the chance, sent across sixty copies of my album, *Everywhere + Nowhere,* and recorded the following message:

Thinking of You
Yo, National Prison Radio listeners. I go by the name of Guvna B. I've been thinking and praying for you all during this tough time. One way that I'm dealing with what's going on right now is reflecting on the fact that this ain't the first tough time I've faced. Coming from where I come from, tough times are a part of life, but I got faith that the way we all got through the tough times of the past will be the same way we get through this. So, faith, perseverance, try to maintain

a positive mindset. One of the people I look up to is Nelson Mandela. He was restricted about where his body could go but he didn't allow his mind to be caged. He kept hope alive and when he left prison, man became president. If we don't allow our minds to be caged, I wonder what we can achieve. Keep your head up, man. Love and prayers, always. Guvna B

When I wrote *Everywhere + Nowhere,* it was a personal journey marking where I am right now, through which I hoped to bring comfort to other people feeling the same way as me. That is my motivation when I write my songs: to communicate how I am feeling in the hope that it resonates with other people.

In the short time since the album dropped, the world has changed almost out of recognition. I haven't heard a plane pass by in days and that alone is a weird thing.

One minute, we're on one track heading in our own direction, and then suddenly, we're all on the same track, talking about the same stories, living the same experiences, lives in disarray from the same event.

That's really big.

So, yeah, I guess what I'm saying is that now, all over the world, we *are* everywhere and nowhere, figuring whether or not to take this opportunity granted to us, to embrace a new way of living, or instead, climb the walls and try to hang on to the familiarity of the old.

I had no idea that there was a life-changing pandemic around the corner when I wrote my album, but somehow my lyrics to the track, 'Everywhere and Nowhere', are as true to now, in this whole new normal, as when I wrote them. I suppose this just goes to highlight how nothing is fixed in time or place, and we just have to trust in God to guide us.

Everywhere and Nowhere

It's been a crazy ten years.
We just try to keep it moving while battling all our fears.
I was on a way to a show with the tank on empty,
    cause my card was in arrears.
Two MOBOs and thirty countries, it's looking a little
    different.
Man, how did we get here?
I was chillin' with the prince in the palace.
Same day we hit five million streams on the album,
But still no radio, still no record deal, still dey don't
    rate me tho.
And still getting guest list texts
The night before my sets and friends still don't pay
    for shows.
Still the token guy in the line-up,
Ticking the diversity box, while getting it hyped up.
Still learning to count my blessings,
But sometimes I'm stressing.
It's like it's never-ending.
I'm grateful for what has happened, but still searching
    for more.
Five albums deep, but still, I re-record.
It's me and Jimmy James in our humble home studio,
Saving up the pennies. Hope we only got a few to go
'Cause we'd love a home for the future flows.
Bless another artist, who wanna make their music go,
But I'm just a rapper with no rich benefactor.
So all I can do is stack up and ask God the route to go.

Tryna pay a mortgage with a newborn son, don't
    know if I can afford it.

Plus my accountant just did the audit:
Great summer, but I been quiet since August.
I'm reminiscing cause one thing that I've learnt is that
God always provides, so I can never forfeit.
But it's easier said than done.
Still just watch me take off cause I walk it like I talk it.
It's like I'm half-rapper, half-worship leader.
Tryna find my place, find my lane, I got circus fever.
The more I see, the more I feel outta place.
I'm not quite Stormzy and I'm not quite Lecrae.
Guess I'll look beneath the surface for faith.
These are songs from heaven,
And it's not a burden, it's grace.
I've been searching for a sermon for days:
One on insecurity and how I'm nervous to say
The truth is, I don't even know what I'm doing, don't
    even know where I'm going.
I just live in the moment and hope
That my future is in your plans and you're on the
    throne.
So uncomfortable with your plans, I know that I'll grow.
You're the maker of the planet
So even if I'm everywhere and nowhere,
I'm fine, cause my Saviour doesn't panic
And he's in control here.

14. THE WAY AHEAD

Suppressing our emotions, acting tough, and using aggression as a form of expression means that men, in particular, are completely ill-equipped to cope with all of the obstacles and challenges that life throws their way.

We might think it is the 'safe' way to be as our masculinity defines us, but the truth is, if we remain in this emotionless state, we can expect knock-on negative consequences on all aspects of our lives, including our relationships, as lack of communication, empathy, and emotions are a sure fire route to conflict.

I have had to learn this the hard way.

For many years, I inhabited three states of mind: passivity, rage, plus joy, in my love of Jesus. Those were my go-to, my comfort zones, and I thought that I was pretty enlightened, someone with my head screwed on the right way. I believed that I was fulfilled by where I was in my life, and even though I was not following a traditional path when it came to a profession, I was achieving in the way that my parents expected me to achieve – earning a living and being true to my purpose.

My parents brought me up to be the way they believed boys should be and by this, I mean to be proud, strong, robust enough to hold myself together, and manly enough never to cry – essential character traits that were further reinforced by the environment I grew up in.

Any sign of weakness on my behalf would make my mum anxious and cause my friends to tease me, and any opportunity my dad and I had to open up and go a layer deeper, we laughed off, favouring silence over honesty.

That's just how life was, and it seemed to work, and would have continued working just fine had it not been for me losing my dad quite out of the blue, with everything I had come to accept as 'normal' crashing down as a result.

In the years since, my brain has undergone a comprehensive rewiring. At first, it wasn't easy to reveal parts of me I had never revealed before. In fact, I am pretty certain that if I had not been in the depths of grief, I would almost certainly never have dared to do so much soul-searching or be truthful about the output.

Now, I can honestly say that not a day goes by without me giving thanks to God for showing me that there is another way to live. It took many months of me staggering around in the dark before I located the light switch; months in which I turned to drink as a release, where complete inertia compromised my marriage and my friendships, and my depression led me to seriously contemplate taking my own life.

It did not need to be so extreme.

Grief, as I like to remind people, is the natural human response to trauma and to loss – and that of many other species. Work with it and it is a healing remedy; fight against it and it is the equivalent of continuously picking at a scab.

I had a loving family and good friends who stood by me, but I chose to deal with my grief on my own. I believed I was being strong by holding it in, but the reality is, anyone can keep stuff bottled up, whereas strength lies in being able to call out for help.

Why?

Because men are human too: not *super*-human, not *semi*-human but *fully* human, meaning we have been wired with the same catalogue of emotions as women, it's just that, due to our conditioning, our emotions have been starved of food and sunlight, and so have become stunted, gnarled, misshapen; and they impede our full growth.

Men are three times more likely to die as the result of suicide than women because men don't

1. Think to ask for help;
2. Want to ask for help;
3. Know how to ask for help;
4. Dare to ask for help; and
5. All of the above.

Equally, boys are far more likely to be permanently excluded from school due to all of the above and to end up in prison, as – yes, you got it – young men are far more likely to commit violent crimes than young women.

Communicating how we feel does not come naturally to many men. I told you, when my dad was dying in hospital, my mum cried, Emma soothed her, but me and my brother were shut off and silent, pacing the corridors, holding it in.

What is more, compared to women, seeking advice for mental health issues or support from a counsellor, is pretty low on many men's list of survival tactics.

I used to be ashamed about being open and honest and so hid my authenticity even from the people who loved me. The problem is, the more I kept locked up, the bigger my problems became, and the less able I was to handle them. If I had only learnt to be true to myself earlier in my life, I would have saved myself a whole load of pain and bad decisions.

This is why I am intent on telling young people to go and get help with the puddles before they turn into floods.

I would love all young people out there, who are battling with their demons, too fearful, shy, embarrassed, worried to let them out, to turn to someone – anyone – and share. It is hard at first, but when you've done it once and you've seen the positive way the world responds, it spurs you on to do it again and again.

I have a genuine belief that by unfastening the chains and wearing your heart on your sleeve, you will find so much joy in the way the world reacts, and a whole load more meaning in how you react to the world.

That has certainly been the case for me.

It was weeks after my dad died before I felt comfortable crying on my own, and months before I dared release that cry out into the open for all the world to see. In fact, it was my cousin who showed me it was okay to dare.

This particular cousin is younger than me but he inspires me. I was standing across from him at his mum's burial. As the coffin was lowered into the ground, he started crying, real crying that took a hold of the head, the shoulders, and heart. Seeing him open up like that released something in me, and before I knew it, I was crying too; the same all-encompassing cry. My cry was partially for my deceased aunt, of course, but mostly, it was for my cousin, because I knew what it must have taken for that strong, proud man to cry out in the open like that.

A few months ago, I cried again. No stopping me now! I was sitting with some of my other cousins talking about our aunt who had passed away (Don't worry; there is nothing sinister to read into this: I just have a lot of ageing aunties) and we were all talking and remembering her. The tears were there, rolling down all of our cheeks, but then one of my cousins said something funny, and we all just burst out laughing. Laughing and crying at the same time … See? I've come a long way.

I thank Emma for showing me that it's fine to cry, because she is such a believer in men showing their emotions. If ever she sees me crying, that sets her off, and once she is off, there's no stopping her. Learning to cry and not being judged for crying has been one of my greatest releases.

So, just in case you haven't picked it up from my many thousands of words: Newsflash – I loved my dad.

He was everything I strive to be: hard-working, laid-back, happy in his skin, and loved by every heart he touched. If I can be half as successful a dad to Ezra as my dad was to me, he will be a blessed boy.

But …

I'm not going to follow in my dad's footsteps with the child-rearing, not totally at least. My dad never had the time or inclination to run spot checks on the state of his mental health, let alone the mental wellbeing of me and my brother. He just needed to know that we had food to eat, a place to live, and books to study. That was his purpose. That was why he lived to work and worked to live. I don't need to work as hard as my dad: whether or not I choose to is another matter, but it's not a necessity. I am in a position in my professional life where I don't need to live hand-to-mouth just to keep afloat. That means I can think more broadly.

Like my dad, I will be strict, because I want Ezra – and any subsequent children – to grow up with clear boundaries, but where I will differ from my dad is, when I am being strict, and Ezra asks, 'Why?' I'm not going to answer, 'Because', and leave it at that.

Sorry, Pops, but it's just not much of an answer. I am going to explain the 'why' to Ezra and then tell him that he can ask me any question that he wants to ask.

He'll grow up going to church, because that is what Emma and I do, but sooner or later, he is going to start wanting to make his own decisions, and that is when I will be there to provide him with all the answers he needs, and an open mind to listen to all his conclusions.

When it comes to eating, I intend to cook a lot of Ghanaian munch because I want my kids to know their roots in their hearts, minds, *and* stomachs. But I'm not going to leave the food sitting on the hob when it's cooked ready for my kids to help themselves.

No way.

When it comes to dining, we are going to do it differently, and by that, I mean we are going to sit around a dining table and engage one another in chat.

It's going to take me a while to get used to this as it's new territory, so I'll let Emma take the lead while I find my feet, but those mealtimes are going to happen. I want my kids to grow up knowing that what they have to say matters, and in order to do that, I'm happy spending my munch-time listening to whatever they've gotta say.

I never doubted my dad's love for me, but I wish that he'd told me he loved me more often. Yeah, he did: right at the very end of his life, he said it: 'I love you.' Hearing those words changed my life, but I had to get to twenty-seven years of age first. I could have done with more reassurance earlier. Don't ask me why, because I don't know. My boy, Ezra, is never going to have to wonder about my love, because I am going to be telling him that I love him every single day of his life.

No joke.

I've started already. He's too young to make sense of what those three words mean, but soon he will know and hopefully, as a consequence, he will feel secure of his place on this earth, and be able to carry himself with all the pride of a boy who knows his daddy loves him. Hopefully, when he gets to be a dad himself, far into the future, he also won't hesitate to bare his heart to his first born son, because we gotta break the cycle and boys need to know.

Boys need to know their daddies love them with an unconditional love.

So yeah, I love you, Ezra Charles Nii-boye Borquaye. My G.

It's funny because one of my greatest pleasures, as I told you before, is finding out about other people's lives and hearing their stories. I learn so much from other people by listening to what they've got to say.

The irony here, though, is that even though my dad was one of the most special people in my life, I never got to hear his story. I never sat him down, like I do with a whole load of people nowadays, and said, 'So, Dad, tell me all about it.'

The truth is – and I feel bad when I think about this – I doubt I would ever have actually made the time to ask him much when he was still alive, as he was never someone who put a huge amount of time aside for idle chat. I am pretty certain if I had initiated the conversation, it would have gone something like this:

'So, Dad, what was it like growing up in Kokomlemle?'

'It was good, son.'

'Any particular memories?'

'One or two.'

'What memories were they?'

'This and that.'

He was an easy man to be with, to sit alongside, and pass the time of day, but a bit trickier to chat to deeply.

What I do know is that if I had time with my dad again, I would never let the opportunity for a conversation pass. If I could sit beside him in the car with him driving me home from the airport, I would fill him in on every single detail of my tour, and ask him in return for every single detail of what he'd been up to while I was away.

And I wouldn't take silence – or laughter – for an answer.

That is what Ezra is going to get. He is going to get his pop talking to him and asking him questions. Basically I am going to annoy him, innit!

So, this is my book: *Unspoken: Toxic Masculinity and How I Faced the Man within the Man*. It's quite a title, isn't it? Perhaps you were expecting some fisticuffs as I battled with the old me, or the literary version of a car chase, as I hit the gas in pursuit of my rage.

That ain't true life though, is it? In reality, what the last few years have taught me is that life is not about getting from A to B, from rags to riches, from obscurity to fame, but about the beautiful struggle in the middle.

There is no such thing as a good life or a bad life, simply what you make of the life you have. Yeah, I know that sometimes it seems hard and like there is nowhere to turn, but when a door seems firmly closed, there is always an unlocked window.

When my dad died, I saw the years without him stretching

ahead of me into the distance, empty and bleak, but then I was reminded with each new day that, thanks to my faith, I was edging that little bit closer to seeing him again.

There is always a bright side, a chance to learn, to listen, to teach, to give thanks, to inspire.

Once upon a time, I didn't think my life would amount to much. I used to hang around my estate trying to earn respect, to fit in, to have people notice me, and then I realized that the only way I was going to see the change I longed for was to *be* that change.

Fast-forward to 2020 and it's sick that it's not streaming figures or ticket sales, trainers or flashy cars that bond me together with the people in my life, but openness and honesty – gifts that God grants us for free.

So, if you were expecting cut-throat drama, you're in the wrong place, as this man is all about the beauty that life has to offer: the joy of fatherhood, love languages with my wife, being a dedicated son, and, hopefully, carrying on doing what matters to me big time, and that is, being a big brother to all my Gs.

Cos remember, for as long as my heart is beating, I'm gonna have your back.

AFTERWORD

Initially, I wasn't sure whether or not to mention the Covid-19 pandemic in this book because it seemed to be all that anyone talked about at the time of writing. And anyway, it might all be over when this book hits the shelves – #unlikely.

But seeing as I've been talking about *Everywhere + Nowhere*, the bittersweet, and two states of mind, it kinda feels unavoidable.

So, first off, when the virus struck, I was completely gutted as I'd had the whole year mapped out and it was gonna be a good 2020! I had my new album dropping, tour dates booked, and a loada tickets sold, so lots of stuff going on – not to mention the fact that these hands *are* made for working, and this man's not good at idle.

So, it took me a while to accept that Covid-19 was even a thing. Even when it became clear that it was banging on our island's door, I tried to fight it and pretend it wasn't that much of a big deal – or at least, if it was happening, it wasn't going to touch me.

I kept busy, going out and about, doing my ting.

Then my wife had a go at me: 'Isaac, this is serious. We've got a baby, and we don't know what the effects of the virus are. We've gotta keep him safe.'

I tried rationalizing it, by telling her that there was no proof that babies got it worse than anyone else, but I didn't really have much to back this up. And anyway, he's my son and undeniably, the most important person in my life.

On 23 March, when the Prime Minister addressed the nation and announced the blanket lockdown, then I knew that it was serious.

No football. No NBA.

My first reaction was to do what I guess nearly every self-employed human being across the world did at pretty much the same moment – panic about what the impact would be on my income, as everything planned for 2020 was being cancelled left, right, and centre.

As someone who likes to be in control, suddenly having the ground disappear from beneath my feet brought the reality home to me that, despite what I told myself, I was *not* the king of my castle after all. In fact, in the face of a deadly virus, man was stranded.

How could something as catastrophic as this happen? So many thousand deaths; so much tragedy; all those families in unbearable grief. I got to sit by my dad's bedside after he died. I got to say goodbye at a huge funeral befitting the man he was. I can barely imagine the pain this virus has brought to so many husbands, wives, sons, and daughters, robbed of saying goodbye due to hospital restrictions, and subject to the severe shock of losing their loved ones so suddenly and unexpectedly.

Sometimes I wonder if the reason my own grief was classified as 'complicated' and led to depression was because of the shock factor of losing my dad. Although I am not in any way underestimating the power of grief when someone has died after a long illness, the speed and unexpected aspect of my dad's death still haunts me. Not being given the chance to prepare for his death, or for any of the subsequent deaths I experienced, has resulted in me now always jumping to the worst conclusion. If I call my mum three times in a few hours and she doesn't pick up, I have to stop myself from jumping in the car and driving over, gripped by fear that she might be lying collapsed on the floor. I have been assured that these responses are very common in such circumstances.

A consequence of the shock means that in the years since, I have flipped into self-preservation mode, whereby I find I am already priming myself for the next tragedy in my life. This sounds quite morbid, but in order to protect myself from the onrush of grief I am likely to experience at my mum's death, for example, I have mapped out all possible scenarios, so that I know, when it happens, I will already be some way into the grieving process.

Also, I have started facing up to my own death. I am a father now, and so I need to think about Ezra's future. That is why I have started to ensure there is money put aside for him. I would never have prepared in this way if my dad's death had not taken me by such complete surprise.

For those whose lives have not been affected directly by Covid-19, something else has emerged from being forced into an unprecedented lockdown, distanced from one another, and prevented from embarking on the pressures of the everyday. And I gotta say, it hasn't all been bad.

In fact, there have been a lot of positives.

For me, ever since Ezra was born, I have been running around, getting my album off the ground, and doing my ting, snatching only precious moments with my family.

Being forced to stop, however, I have found myself settling comfortably into downtime, spending quality hours with Ezra, watching every tiny little change as each new day passes, and also getting to know my wife. Yeah, she's a mum now, and before, I hadn't really taken the time to acknowledge her in this role. But it's enabled a whole new quality love language.

Of course, that's me speaking. I'm not sure how she's found it with me hanging around the whole time. If you were to ask her, she might say that life with Isaac can be *bittersweet*.

The side of me most people see is Businessman Isaac, looking forward, working towards my goals, inspiring, persevering. Work is my release, particularly when I'm up on stage. For the forty-five minutes or so that that lasts, nothing else in my life matters. I feel completely free.

The Isaac she sees, though, is Mr Passive. I like to call it 'laid-back', but I know she calls it 'passive'. I can stop work at any time and take a few days out to chill: that's why I can throw myself at it. But when you're a husband and a father, it's a full-time position. I think Emma would be happier if, in my full-time role, I had a bit more oomph, made a few more decisions, took life by the horns. I'm trying because I know it means a lot to her, but it doesn't come naturally.

What I can tell you is that, as a consequence of all that we have been through in the course of our marriage, we are definitely stronger now than we were when we started out. Emma's parents have a super loving relationship, and so I think Emma came into our marriage thinking that all marriages were like her parents', and we would have the same seemingly flawless union. It's not been a smooth run though. With my dad dying, and me dipping into the drinking, my good friends passing, and all the arguing before we learnt about resolving our conflicts, and now the pandemic, we've had a fair share of real life thrown at us.

That we have got through so much, however, has proved

to us that we are not going to give up on each other.

Another one of Emma's diary entries shows you the bumpy ride (27 August 2017):

> Last night, me and Isaac had another argument and I felt hopeless. I wanted love and comfort so much but right now I need God to be my comfort and God to be the object of my love and I need to see our relationship through God's eyes. For what it shall be! We will be stronger and understand one another better, we will love each other more greatly, we will communicate better. Strength and wholeness will come. God will restore us.

And these are some lyrics I wrote one month into the pandemic:

> Even on the worst days, I know there's blessing to count.
> And that's after I checked my bank account, never stressing though.
> The beauty of community is we stick together,
> through the rain, and no matter the weather, I know we'll be okay.
> Prayers to everybody shouting SOS.
> And prayers to everybody in the NHS.
> Forever in our hearts, I know the storm will pass
> Stay safe, stay well, stay blessed.

Over time, I have got past the many questions I had for God during this pandemic, and I'm beginning to trust in his plan. He has shown me that all the stuff I considered essential to my life – a steady income stream, maintaining a hold on my business, eating Nando's chicken daily – can be whipped away super quick, and we need to root ourselves in something deeper and more meaningful, that is solid and here to stay; and that, for me, is valuing the time I spend with my loved ones.

Oh yeah, don't worry, I did manage to source some Nando's, so even bigger thumbs-up (picture 22).

> Can't wait to grab my walking stick, head over to my favourite chair, get my grandkids round the fire, take off my flat cap, and tell them the story of how I managed to get a cheeky Nandos during a worldwide pandemic without breaking any social distancing rules.
> (Instagram, 28 April 2020)

So yeah, there's a whole load of bittersweet going on right now and the world feels like it's everywhere and nowhere, as we all try and figure out who we are, and where we are in the new 'normal'. No doubt what was tough before is going to get even tougher, as the Government figures out a way of getting the economy back on its feet. And it's going to be the most deprived young people that bear the brunt.

Of course, I know that a lot of what I have just said about the positives that relate to pandemic living will be out of touch with some of you who might be living in fear for your safety. Maybe by not being able to go to school or work, you've been forced indoors with an abusive family member, with limited options for places to hide. Maybe you have been beaten up, and are living scared. Or, maybe you've got a gang hanging out on your doorstep; hounding you, threatening you, and with no school to keep you apart you've had to face them every day.

My thoughts are with you all. I'm praying for you and trust in God to keep you safe.

ACKNOWLEDGEMENTS

Whenever I write something substantial, I have to say 'thank you' to Ms Aanonson: thanks for telling me that I was a good writer and making me believe in myself when I was unaware of my talents. If all primary school head teachers were like you, I'm sure more kids would know that they're worth something.

Special thanks to the team at HarperCollins. You've done a fantastic job of amplifying what I'm passionate about and it warms my heart to know that, because of your hard work, more people might be inspired to fight toxic masculinity.

To my team – Abby Arons, Loretta Andrews, Mez Gauton, Sam Gill, Jason Coker, Luke English, Hannah Celnikier, Sam Jennings, Joe Osborne, Ian Dutt, James Moodie, Andrea Edmondson, and Karim Khan – thanks for giving your time and effort towards making my dreams come true.

To the powerful women in my life – Mum and Emma; I'm not sure where I'd be without your influence. You are two of the strongest individuals I know. Mum, the fact you're still standing strong, and trying your best to see the blessings in life, is really inspiring. I know Dad would be very proud of you and we all believe that you have the strength to keep going. Emma, I know when Dad passed away lots of people were worried about me, but often underestimated how tough it must have been for you as a comforter. Thanks for standing strong and being a rock when I needed you to be.

Ezra, my first-born son, you can't even talk properly yet, but with everything I do, just know that I think about how it impacts you. The great thing about art is that it never dies. Long after I'm gone this book will still be alive. Whenever you read it, I'm hoping it'll help you along your journey. You got this! The same goes for you, Joel: I'm proud of the man you've become, and I couldn't have wished for a better little brother – it's a pleasure making all the mistakes so you can learn from me!

Big up the mandem: too many names to mention, but a lot of this book came out of conversations we've had. Thanks for allowing me to be vulnerable. There's not much better than genuine brotherhood.

Dad, there're not enough words to express the love and gratitude I have for you – so I wrote a book with 70,000! Thank you.

Finally, I have to give thanks to God. I'm not going to lie, I don't always understand your ways, but even on the worst of days, I recognize that there're always blessings to count. Whenever I'm in the middle of a storm, I can't always see how good things can come out of it, but this book is a prime example that it's possible.

Love to everyone who took the time to read this book, and to everyone who follows me on social media or buys my music. I don't think you realize just how much you mean to me.

Forever grateful.
Guv